Behind Those

streets of London

A Novella

(An Amanda Green Novella Book 1)

By Amanda Green

Dear Simone,
I hope you enjoy reading this as much as I enjoyed writing it. It's my favourite book so far.
Amanda Green x
Oct 16
;)

This book contains some offensive language

Suitable for adults only

This book is a work of fiction

This book copyright ©Amanda Green

ISBN-13: 978-1511847537

First edition published 2014 by Amanda Green

This edition published 2015 by Amanda Green

Copyright of the text produced herein remains the property of the writer and permission to publish is gratefully acknowledged by the author

All rights reserved

No parts of this publication may be reproduced, stored in a retrieval system, or transmitted in any form, by any means, electronic, mechanical, photocopying, recording or otherwise without prior permission of the copyright owner.

Cover art and design by Aidana WillowRaven

For Michael

Strength and Love got us through

xxxxxxx

Some of the reviews so far, for 'Behind Those Eyes'…

5* *"The highest point of this novella, for me, is that the author gives a voice to people who are mostly unheard, unseen, or rejected, silenced. She brings to our attention the reality of their hard and suffered lives, making the readers start to pay more attention to those nameless faces we may see every day asking for money. They all have a story, they all have a past, they all are human beings too, and we should never treat them like less than that."*

5* *""Behind Those Eyes" by Amanda Green is a moving and fascinating story that highlights the problem of homelessness in Britain from a personal perspective.*
One of the main characters observes a homeless man being 'moved along' by the police and that scene moves her and stays with her for some time…

It is a big issue handled with sensitivity, great humanity and warmth and very satisfying when the other sub plots fall into place of the big picture. Highly recommended."

5* "In style this is one of those stories I used to seek out on the New Yorker website. It's rough, with a shot of reality and definitely makes you stop to think a lot. Amanda has a good eye for nuances on the streets of London. Even though I have lived there and would have my own stories to tell, her observations seem authentic and much more local."

5* "I read this wondering what Amanda would make of homelessness and the homeless, having been street homeless myself for a number of years when I was much younger. The story line felt more than legit even after it started to get twisted, and having been in some extremely unlikely situations and outlandish opportunities myself totally get that part of the story too... Unable to put it down. I totally got the *humanity of it too... a fantastic read with excellently true to life characters. Well done Amanda"*

5* "I could not put this book down and read it in one sitting ... Amanda Green keeps you thinking all the way through with her twists and turns ... The characters are wonderfully and realistically portrayed ... this author has a marvellous talent for raw real world story telling ... five star Novella without question"

5* ""Well done Amanda Green! Well done indeed!" For where some writers might choose this difficult topic to teach or preach you showed us the heart of the matter from the inside out and back again!"

4* "I really enjoyed this story. It kept me interested throughout. I liked the way the author switched between characters and narrators so that the story was told from more than one point of view. It shows great skill that the author was able to tell the tale from each of the characters' perspectives while *keeping the prose flowing and holding the reader's attention.*

The book deals with subjects such as depression, homelessness, and family relationships. It's a thought-provoking read and very well constructed. With the main character's sections being written in the first person it felt almost like reading a diary in parts, which made for an engrossing read.

There are a couple of excellent unexpected twists."

THE BEGINNING

So, here I am in Prêt A Manger. I've just stuffed myself on a tuna baguette and tomato soup and am now onto my cappuccino. I got a free muffin too, but I can't eat that. It is busy in here. I got a table by myself and am sitting here happily watching the world go by. Perhaps I should do this more often. I think it's inspiring because of all the noise and people. There is music playing in the background, but the hum of conversation is so overpowering, if you tried to concentrate, you wouldn't know which to listen to. A homeless person (at least he looks homeless) outside was being clocked by police earlier. Whilst here supping on my hot tasty soup, he was out there barely able to get up from the concrete floor. What sort of an existence is that? I am lucky. Am I? Maybe he is happier than me – maybe not. Where does he go to the toilet? What does he eat and drink? How does he get his money? What a state to get into, but it is rife here in London.

As I leave the café, I hear one of the two policemen mention his name 'Malcolm'. I begin to think about why Malcolm is on the street, living like that, taking upheaval from the Metropolitan Police. If I were to sit there, they wouldn't move me along, but they obviously know him. I watch him stare at them for a moment, before landing his right hand on the pavement beside him as he rolls over and begrudgingly kneels in front of them.

"OK, Malcolm, just a bit further mate" says the skinny, po-faced policeman.

"Alright, I'm coming aren't I?" Malcolm protests in a gruff voice, through a mouth in a face that looks to be tainted with sadness.

I notice his stubble, a little greying, as is his brown hair, but he has a full head of hair, fairly short and messy. He looks dishevelled but not totally unhealthy. In fact, he does have good skin. He is dressed in a thick black and dirty overcoat, baggy brown trousers and big black boots, scuffed and worn down at the heels. He has a stripy, thick woolly scarf wrapped twice round his neck, and he looks around fifty years old.

"In your own time" says the other policeman – this time a tall, big built chap - with a sarcastic slight.

I feel angry, I want to go over there, tell them to stop telling the poor man to move. I want to give him some money, some help, a place to stay, to clean up; anything really. I want to interfere, but I cannot. I don't like confrontation.

I also don't want to fund the man's next *Tennents Extra* or *White Lightning*, which I know a lot of people on the street drink, for cheapness... and most likely for comfort.

My eyes cannot divert to the hustle bustle on the street around me; the bright lights of the theatre, the sounds… I am stunned, and I feel I want to know more about this guy. But I cannot. I need to just leave it alone. I have enough on my plate.

Malcolm finally gets to his feet, wobbling and he staggers off.

"Bye Malcolm" I say silently and watch him go.

***

Malcolm was sitting comfortably on the pavement, amongst it all on Victoria Street, when the *Old Bill* came and made him move on. It's something he's used to, and so are the Police, but he still moaned as he tried to find his feet to a standing position, albeit wobbly. It's the boots.

"Yeah, yeah" he said as he wandered off aimlessly, talking to strangers along the way.

"Hello there, spare a pound for the needy?" he said over and over as he passed numerous people of all creeds, sizes and statures.

No-one gave him a penny. He's better off sitting down, he knew that. And he'd be better off being a woman when it comes to gaining sympathy and donations, he knew that too. But, he is what he is, and he continued to ask.

Finding a nice, covered, shop doorway to sit in, and still in the 'busy' area, he settled down for the night. It was early, but it didn't matter to him; he had no place to be, no one to see and nothing to do, and if it rained, he would stay dry. Perfect!

He threw down his old, tatty rucksack, with everything he now owned in it, and pulled out his dark blue, damp, sleeping bag. It was cold, but he was used to it and at least the rain had stopped. He thought about the weather like most people, but he wouldn't see a forecast on TV or think about whether to take an umbrella out with him; he just took each moment as it came. Sometimes it was good, mostly it was rubbish.

He spent another hour or so asking passers' by for donations. His stomach was grumbling, but that was just normal. His efforts reaped £3.54 which was a good day. He counted it up, wanting to go buy some alcohol, maybe food, in that order, but his desire to keep the doorway occupied by his own being, and keeping the warmth in his sleeping bag, was enough to make him stay. He knew it was a good bedding down place. And he was very tired. The night before he hadn't slept much at all…

And so, he settled down to sleep, as passers' by went forth to enjoy theatre productions, pubs, nightclubs, or their journeys home.

***

That night was a living nightmare for Malcolm, and that's saying something, since he was used to a life that was similar to a bad dream…

***

When I reach home, I am suddenly overcome with the reality of what I have; a home, for starters, a kitchen, a lounge, a TV, food in the cupboards and a fridge and freezer. I suddenly see everything I have.

And like a fast spreading virus, thoughts of Malcolm and what he is doing take over. Throughout the evening, I also become unable to concentrate and keep thinking about what I have – from the food I eat, to the hot cup of tea I drink, to the freshly washed and aired dressing gown I put on. I feel guilt washing through me; and all because I saw that man today; Malcolm. OK, I've seen people who live on the streets before, but I've usually been too busy to notice them before, or been too untrusting to believe they are really living like that. So, I've been ignorant, I guess.

I don't live in a palace, it's just a small, one bedroom flat, but if I halved what I spend each month, like rent, food, bills, haircuts, the occasional dress or top, then I feel sure both of us could live somewhere – a bed sit each say. So, why is Malcolm on the streets? Why are there people on the streets? It's 2014; this doesn't seem right to me.

I decide to 'google it' 'How many people are homeless in the UK' I type…

***

The next morning, Malcolm was looking for cigarette butts, as his priority, although he did search bins for food when he passed them. He shuffled along with his rucksack over one shoulder, dragging his feet, not because he couldn't walk properly, but because he couldn't be bothered. He was bedraggled physically and mentally most days and this day is no exception. Occasionally, if he got to drink enough *Tennents Super*, he'd get a fuzzy feeling in his head and those were the better days.

He scoured the uneven pavement for butts, and he saw nothing of the vast array of people rushing past him, with their headphones on, staring into their phones, chatting to someone next to them. He was on a mission. He crouched down slowly when he spotted a butt and picked it up between his dirty, stumpy fingers. A middle aged lady passed, dressed in a red suit, with her coiffured blonde locks bouncing as she walked on her black high heels. She momentarily glanced at his hands, staring at his dirt filled fingernails to see what he was doing. She screwed her beautifully made up face up into a frown, in a look of disgust, and walked on.

Eleven butts worth down the long, busy, London road, and something else took Malcolm's attention from his search.

"That's disgusting! What the fuck is wrong with him, dirty old man!"

The voice seemed to be that of a young lad, and as Malcolm looked up, this assumption was qualified. He was saying this to his friend, who went forth to tell him that sometimes shit happens in life, and people like him end up like that.

"Bollocks!" said the first chap.

They carried on walking, arguing the point, their voices trailing off into the distance. Malcolm was stood, almost like he was paralysed. Nothing much hurt Malcolm; it didn't pay to let anyone or anything hurt you mentally on these streets. But, those comments sparked something in his brain, and he kept repeating the words they'd said over and over in his mind, mumbling as he did.

"Shit happens. Ha, it certainly does young lad!" He said out loud, even though they were long gone by then.

He turned round to find an empty shop with a big 'To Let' sign on the shop front. It was safe to be near those, as no-one would come out and make him move. The people that worked in shops that were open were not very appreciative of Malcolm's presence in front of their windows.

He slumped to the floor, still holding the last couple of butts he'd picked up. The rest were in his left hand coat pocket. The right pocket had a massive hole in it. Twiddling the butts in his fingers, he repeated *Shit happens*.

"Ha! Doesn't it just!" He shouted. A few passers' by glanced towards him, but most people walked on, oblivious to his statement.

"It's always best to keep looking forward, one day at a time" He'd tell his fellow homeless crowd. "I never think back on my life – I find it too painful to remember what I have lost, who I have lost, and the comforts I used to enjoy". Many of them had been living like it for a lot longer than Malcolm, but he had more to say and he liked to get them talking. He was basically an educated, intelligent man, but when anyone appreciated him to that effect verbally, he'd laugh. Not real laughter. Not the laughter that comes from deep inside your belly, not laughter that comes from giggling, this laughter was purely dismissive.

"If you can't laugh at yourself, who can you laugh at eh?" he'd say.

However, right here, right now, was different. What that lad said would not leave him and his brain forced him to physically stop and give in to thoughts from the past; his own and those of his fellow homeless street friends. "Shit happens" he was still mumbling.

He watched a few people pass him and asked a random couple if they could spare any change, but they ignored him, walking on as if they hadn't heard him, when he knew they had. "Have a lovely day" he called behind them. He did mean it. He was a polite man, and begging had not come easy to him…

As the outside world disappeared from his view, his mind concentrated on what he could see from his memories – snippets of moving pictures, like being at the cinema; all the characters talking, moving and playing out a story.

He hadn't been on the streets all that long; it's just that he'd become used to it quickly. *There's no place for an inflated ego or too much pride when needs must!*

Anyone could find themselves in this position he thought suddenly, but, as his eyes moistened and his chin quivered, he quickly decided he wouldn't allow himself to ponder – that could be the end of him on these streets and he had to keep on.

"No can do" he told himself abruptly, and as he came back to the 'moment' he could feel his stomach lurching through hunger, all the aches and pains settling back into his joints and muscles, and he could feel the cold breeze skimming the pavement and whipping up into his face. Back to reality… He thought of that 'Soul2Soul' song, 'Back to Life' as he went forth on his next mission – to find food in those bins out there!

***

Seventy one miles away from the skyscrapers and noise of Victoria Street, London, where Malcolm shuffled through the streets, Thomas jovially chatted to his sister, Liz in his kitchen.

It's the second time they'd seen each other that week, but before that, they hadn't met up for two whole years. Liz had been away in Africa, helping to tutor school children in poverty stricken areas. She had only just returned ten days prior.

They had missed each other, but commitments had always come first, not a trip to Africa for Thomas or a holiday away from her work for Liz. They had a lot of respect for loyalty; they had been brought up to appreciate it.

A hot cup of tea in her hand, Liz told Thomas that she suddenly wishes Jonathan was there too. They were always so close, her two brothers and her.

"I know" replied Thomas with a heavy sigh "me too" he looked at the floor, contemplating for a moment the vision of his brother, smiling and strutting round full of himself.

"Do you still have the photo book?" Liz interrupted the silence and Thomas' daydream.

"Erm, yeah, I think so… it's up in the spare room I think"

"Shall we take a…"

"Yes!" Thomas now butted in "Let's"

He placed his mug of tea on a coaster, on the oak dining table and disappeared out of the kitchen in a flash.

"Ooh" Liz mused out loud, rubbing her hands together.

She pulled out a chair that had been tucked under the oak table, and sat down, drumming her fingers on the table in quick sequence as she waited.

"Got them!" a muffled shout came from Thomas upstairs.

Liz took a sip of her tea and placed the side of the mug against her left cheek, warming her face as she let out a soft "Ahh"

Thomas bounded into the kitchen hugging a large, blue silk covered photo album to his chest. He laid it on the table carefully and pulled a chair out for himself, lifting it to place next to Lizzy so they could see the photos together. As he went to open it, she touched his hand softly and smiled at him. He smiled back at her and pulled the cover open.

"Right, here we go" he said.

***

The next day…

***

I couldn't bring myself to go to work this morning. I never have a day off, so it's not as if I will be in trouble, and it's not a habit I wish to start, but I couldn't sleep.

When I was actually asleep I watched myself cold, dirty and starving, laying in a gutter with not a penny to my name. I woke in a cool sweat, made a cup of tea, drank it, warmed up and got back into bed. This happened twice, the only difference being that the dream was slightly different. In the second dream, someone was calling to me as I lay in a doorway. It sounded like my mum, soothing and kind, but I couldn't make out the words, only my name "Sophie, Sophie" in a slow gentle voice. But, I couldn't hear anymore, I couldn't move and I couldn't wake from slumber even though it was freezing cold in the doorway. I think I was dying.

I finally get out of bed with the alarm. I feel like I have been in some kind of war overnight, both physically and mentally, and my body seems rooted to the house.

I am stressed again but don't know why.

I make coffee and sit at the kitchen table, in a kind of daze, my hands hugging the mug, until my palms burn with the heat, pulling me from my day dreams. What was I just thinking? I can't remember. I just can't remember. I decided to clean – *that will stop all this thinking.*

So, here I am scrubbing the floor of the kitchen. I've vacuumed every room, changed the duvet cover, pillow cases and sheets on my bed, emptied every cupboard and cleaned each interior before putting it all back. I've disinfected every surface of the kitchen and bathroom, tidied every towel and everything else on my cleaning check list. I still go through it all in my mind, over and over. Just to make sure I don't forget anything. *It is nice to get all these tasks completed today* I tell myself.

As I scrub I feel a release; not physically, but mentally. It's like I'm scrubbing my brain and I want it to be totally shining, but for the brain I know it's not the surface that needs to be worked upon, it's what's inside it and that is another matter altogether.

***

"It's best to give homeless people food or soft drinks, not money, as they can spend money on drugs or alcohol but if you give food or drink then at least they eat or drink".

***

"Alright Malcolm"

A familiar voice greeted Malcolm as he slowly packed his sleeping bag into a tube to fix to his rucksack.

Malcolm turned his head round but didn't stop his packing. "Oh, hi mate" he replied, to the tall, skinny, fellow homeless man behind him.

"How're ya keeping?" asked the man.

"So, so" said Malcolm. "How about you, Robbie?"

"Not bad" said Robbie, letting out a sigh "can't complain."

It was reminiscent of a couple of female friends meeting up in the supermarket whilst in the middle of their shopping list or waiting at the school gates for their children to come out Blah, blah, blah… Except these two were grubby looking men on the streets of London.

"Gonna catch a beer?" asked Robbie.

"Yep, sure thing" replied Malcolm quickly, throwing his bag on his shoulder.

Just as he span round, another homeless man walked by, looking at the concrete pavement as he went.

"Hi" said Malcolm to the man, but the man just glanced up and grunted, so he turned to Robbie and shrugged "Oh well…"

"Don't worry about it, he's a bit…" Robbie stopped talking as he twirled his right index finger towards his head.

"Oh yeah, so what, is he not well… in the head?" Malcolm asked.

"You could say that!" Robbie replied "like many on these streets. Probably like me!"

"Tell me more" invited Malcolm.

The rest of the afternoon was spent in Hyde Park drinking a couple of beers.

***

I check my watch, its two o'clock on the dot, and still no sign of Malcolm. I've been sitting here for one hour thirty five minutes now, hoping to catch him. I want to talk to him. Or should I rephrase that – I *need* to talk to him. I need to know more about him. Maybe if I walk I'll have a better chance of seeing him. Or should I stay here? Oh I don't know, maybe I should just go home and forget all about it, get an early night to make sure I get into work tomorrow. All these maybes; I hate my indecision of late. Maybe I need more pills. Maybe I need more than that.

I rise from my seat in the coffee shop, pull on my quilted coat, my woolly scarf and grab my handbag. I'm going to take a walk.

I head towards Victoria Station.

***

Malcolm paused in front of an electrical shop. An image on the multiple TV's in the window catches his attention.

"What is it?" Robbie asked.

"Oh nothing" replied Malcolm, as he continued to watch the news about the storms in the UK "Let's go"

Sitting in the park, Malcolm was full of questions for Robbie.

"So, how long have you been on the streets then mate?"

Robbie paused, looked up to the sky and turned down his mouth in deep thought for a moment.

"Erm, well, about four years"

"Oh yeah, what were you doing before that then?"

"I was a chef, but then everything went wrong, I got a divorce, she took loads of my money and then I spent the rest on booze. And here I am." Robbie smiled a wry smile, as he finished his sentence.

"Oh" Malcolm thought for a moment. "So, mate, do you think you'll get off the streets, be a chef again?"

"A chef; well, I doubt that very much. I can't see a way back to all that stuff"

"What, you'd rather stay out here, doing all this?"

"I'm alright" Robbie tried to convince himself.

"Mmm, so where are you from?" asked Malcolm.

"What about you? Why all the questions today?"

"Oh yeah, well, I know, I'm just interested mate"

"Right" said Robbie slowly. "Well, I'm from Surrey; Marlow to be exact"

"Nice" replied Malcolm "I mean, so I heard"

"Yep, it was nice... Until the shit hit the fan"

Malcolm said nothing, but continued to look into Robbie's eyes as he took a swig from his beer can, so Robbie continued.

"I was a good chef; a great chef. I earned a lot of money; and then…" his mouth quivered lightly as he tailed off and three large tear drops left his eyes and ran down his face. "Agh!" he continued loudly, rubbing his eyes roughly with the back of right forearm. "Enough of all that shit! What about you?"

"Me?"

"Yeah you"

"Erm, well not much to say; I lost everything and now I'm on the streets."

"Yeah? So how long have you been without a proper home then?"

"Oh, like you; I lose count'

"Huh! Drugs? Drink? What was it that fucked you up?"

"Drink" said Malcolm, a little distracted. "Do you ever use a hostel? They are a nightmare to get in. I've never liked queues"

"Oh yeah, sometimes… They don't allow drink though, and vet you on the door so I have to stay pretty sober to get in. It's alright. Mostly, I prefer the freedom of the outdoors"

"Freedom?" laughed Malcolm. He said it again, only more thoughtfully "Freedom? Yes I suppose there is that to it. Do you feel free then Robbie?"

"Huh, well not really, as I can't get far, and the *Old Bill* get down my throat, but I am free still. No nagging woman, no needy children, no… and no fucking money, that's the problem. People seem to be giving less these days"

"Why'd ya think that is?"

"I don't know" Robbie said, carefully. "I guess they just don't care"

"Or maybe they don't have as much to spare?" offered Malcolm.

"Well, whatever it is, Malcolm, it doesn't help me"

"What about helping yourself?" Malcolm had gone too far with his questions.

"What is this, the fucking Spanish inquisition? Are you up to something Malcolm, you nosey bastard?" Robbie got up from the wooden bench seat, and began shouting. "Trying to wear me down are…"

"No!" interrupted Malcolm quickly "No, not at all! I was just asking my friend, that's all"

"Asking? Well, I think you've done enough asking for one day, eh mate?" Robbie pronounced the word mate in keeping with the word and emotion of *hate*.

"Yes, yes, alright. What say we go and check out the cafe area? The bins are usually good round there aren't they?" offered Malcolm.

"Yeah, OK, finally you see sense"

***

It was 11.45pm before Liz left Thomas' house. "Lucky I drive eh Thomas?" she said as she left "I wouldn't want to be on those streets at this time of night.

"Quite right" Thomas agreed. "You drive carefully, and I'll see you Sunday, OK?"

"Oh yes, I sure will. Sweet dreams Thomas" she said as she kissed her brother on his left cheek.

They had a short hug and she left. He watched her back out of the driveway in her white

VW Beetle and waved her off as she accelerated up the road.

Thomas sighed, and wandered into the kitchen to pour himself a cold glass of mineral water from the fridge. He took it upstairs, placed it on his bed side table, set the alarm on the clock next to it, cleaned his teeth in the bathroom and fell into bed. Just as he began thinking about the conversation he'd just had with his sister, he fell deeply into sleep.

It only took seven minutes for Liz to arrive at her house, since the roads were so clear late at night, but she was not as tired as her brother. She actually felt quite wired actually, like she'd downed a few caffeine energy drinks or something. Her mind was whizzing…

Looking at photos of Jonathan always upset her, but today she just hadn't been able to get far into the photo album without breaking down into tears. Thomas had consoled her, and they had decided to watch a couple of old films instead – Gone with the Wind and Calamity Jane – which they both liked. The films and tasty snacks and dinner that Thomas had prepared had been enjoyable and had taken her mind off her sadness, but in parting, those thoughts had gate crashed Liz's brain once again.

Where is he? What is he doing? Why did he leave? Will I ever see him again?

She poured herself a large brandy, went to bed and attempted to read her current book *The Diary of Anne Frank* but she couldn't focus, and eventually fell into slumber after half hour of reading the same sentence over and over, still not taking in what the paragraph really said.

***

Malcolm and Robbie went their separate ways later on in the evening, and after a few hours sat on the cold floor in front of the shops asking the people walking past them if they had any spare change, they both bedded down for the night within an hour of each other. It was too cold to stay up all hours; far too cold.

Twenty sixth of bloody January mused Malcolm to himself as he lay on the hard floor. His legs ached, his shoulders hurt, he felt pretty sick in his gut, most likely from the cold pizza he'd rescued from the bin from earlier and shared with Robbie. It was almost tasty, but had been very cold and certainly not fresh. He wrote some things on a little notebook he carried with him, downed a bit of strawberry milkshake he'd found along the way, dumped by the kerb, and was asleep within half hour, once he'd warmed himself by breathing into his sleeping bag relentlessly.

***

Robbie woke early morning, before the bin men had even come round. It was time to move on anyway, so he packed up his bedding and stumbled off up the road. He smelt coffee wafting from an Italian café as he wandered by. He stopped in his tracks, inhaling the aroma deeply. A lady in a suit passed and offered him a pound. He took it and thanked her profusely, while she continued, hurrying to work most likely. It wasn't enough to buy a coffee but it was a great start to the day. Robbie sat down and thought about his new friend, Malcolm, who he'd only met a couple of weeks ago. He seemed nice; too nice in fact. And interested; maybe too interested. He thought about all the questions from the day before and more of his past came flooding back to him. He'd not thought about it for a long time, always dismissing thoughts as they arrived. *No point living in the past* he'd always told himself; *you're a new man now*.

But now; now he couldn't shove those memories away into the back of his mind. The more he tried to, the faster the visions came; of his family, his friends, his ex-wife, his children. His children he'd adored; that he still adored, really.

He got up with a start and decided to go find his new friend.

✦ ✦ ✦

Meanwhile, Malcolm had been sick in the night, moved onto another doorway, slept for just two hours and was now wandering up Victoria Street, amongst the slowly growing number of pedestrians, looking for Robbie.

***

It didn't take long before Robbie and Malcolm met again. They hadn't bedded down far apart in the first place, and hadn't wandered far this early morning either.

"Hey, man!" Malcolm shouted and Robbie turned round at the familiar voice.

"Alright mate?" he asked.

"Yep, I'm alright mate" Malcolm tried to hide his smile, which wanted to be a huge beaming grin, by coughing.

"Have another cigarette" said Robbie with a smirk.

"Yeah, I will, when I can find a few butts" replied Malcolm.

"Got any more questions for me today?" asked Robbie, hoping the answer would be yes.

"Well, er, no, I didn't mean to pry too much yesterday, I was just trying to…"

"No worries mate" butted in Robbie "I think I quite liked it" he announced.

"Hah! Well that's a surprise mate" Malcolm was genuinely surprised, but inside he was very excited.

"Want to ask me anymore?"

"Well, yeah, as a matter of fact I do – it will while the time away eh"

***

Back at work after my day off, I feel like an alien; awkward isn't the word. My boss said good morning to me, and smiled, but it feels odd having time off yesterday that wasn't part of my holiday. Maybe I'll go to see him and tell him to take it as holiday. Yes that's what I'll do…

I knock on his door timidly "Come in" he responds in his well-spoken voice.

"Hi, erm…"

"Take a seat, relax, what can I do for you, Miss Taylor?"

"Well… I wasn't in yesterday and um… I just wasn't feeling well, but I, er, I do feel bad about it, so wondered if we could put it down as holiday. I never take a day off sick…"

"I know" he interrupts.

"Yes, well, er, could we? Put it down as holiday?"

"Absolutely… not! I'm not having you taking holiday just because you felt unwell for one day. That would be preposterous! I couldn't possibly. Now, Miss Taylor I very much appreciate you coming in to see me today, and I respect your ability to work so well and with no sick days in the three years you have worked for me, but everyone gets unwell at one time or another. What would be the point of coming into work if you felt rough? You might make mistakes, you might make yourself more unwell, and I do not want that! Do you understand?"

"Oh yes, Mr Banks, I do understand, yes, it was silly of me, and now I am wasting time when I should be working, and you, Mr Banks, could be working too." I am shaking and very aware my tone sounds like a desperate child who is telling their mummy they did take a biscuit without asking and will never do it again. I let out a little giggle as I think this, and Mr Banks smiles at me.

"It's OK Miss Taylor, it's perfectly OK. Now I do have a few things I must do this morning, so if you'd excuse me" he says kindly.

"Yes, yes of course, Mr Banks, I'll get back to my desk"

"Have a good day… Sophie"

"And you Mr Banks, and you" I shuffle out of his office and close the door behind me, taking in a deep breath and breathing out a sigh of relief as I walk towards my desk.

What is wrong with me? Why do I feel and act like a child? Why do I feel so nervous? Maybe I should go to the doctor. Yes I will, in my own time.

At lunch time I make a doctor's appointment for Friday afternoon at two. That is only two days away and soon enough for me. *Maybe I shall feel better by then.*

***

Malcolm and Robbie had a great chat. Robbie found out that Malcolm is fifty four years old, has been married, and had two children, a boy and a girl of eleven and eighteen respectively. But every time Robbie asked more questions, Malcolm changed the subject back to Robbie.

"Ah, my life's boring, not much to tell" was one of his excuses, or "Come on, your life is so interesting, it's *you* we need to talk about"

Although Robbie momentarily thought that perhaps Malcolm had something to hide, he brushed off the thought as he was, by then, very enthused to talk about his own past; his successes and disappointments, his loves, his hates, his family, his friends.

Robbie was now forty nine, divorced (a very messy and expensive one) and had lost all contact with his children just before he ended up on the streets. His children would now be fourteen (his daughter, Francine), twelve (his son, Timothy) and nine (his second son, James) but he hadn't seen them for four years.

"So clever they were. I bet they still are!" Robbie enthused, smiling.

They were sat on the concrete pavement on Buckingham Palace Street, a busy London road, occasionally putting out their hand and asking passers' by for any change, a few of which flipped coins in their direction or handed them a pound or so, and the conversation flowed.

Robbie skipped all his school and home stuff, and mostly wanted to talk about his later years, meeting his beautiful, hazel eyed, dark haired wife,

Rosie, when he was just twenty one and how he had wooed her with his cookery skills, which she had often sampled at his restaurant after hours, when they'd share late night dinners and a glass of wine.

Robbie had fallen in love with Rosie almost as soon as they had first met, in a crowded bar in Camden. It had been a busy Saturday night and Rosie had been caught in a crowd that was swaying to the beats of the rock band playing, and as she'd tried to wrestle her way to the bar she was almost spat out of the crowd right into Robbie's chest!

Robbie laughed softly as he remembered their meeting and he turned to Malcolm and solemnly said "I loved her. I still love her. But I fucked it up. It was all my fault"

Regardless, he continued to tell Malcolm about the good times; the parties, the romance, the first kiss, everything he could remember, and the time passed very quickly. It was dark by the time he was explaining how he'd managed to own his own restaurant. Then it was time to move on. They hadn't nearly enough money to buy food, so they went their separate ways for the evening, and made an arrangement to meet the next day at the park.

This whole conversation left Malcolm in deep thought.

***

I didn't make any dinner tonight. I just didn't feel up to it. In fact what have I done? I put the TV on for a while, but got bored and turned it off again. I fed the fish. I think I fed the fish. Did I feed the fish? I'm not sure. OK I'm going to feed the fish now, just in case. I fed the cat. Yes I definitely fed the cat. If I hadn't fed the cat, he'd be jumping on me or meowing for it. Yes, he's been fed. What else? Erm, oh I had a quick look at the Daily Mail, but every story seemed to be depressing and upsetting. Oh balls, I'm going to bed, better I'm asleep than keep going over this monologue of my day!

***

I couldn't sleep. I kept tossing and turning, thinking endlessly about all kinds of things; the homeless man, Malcolm, my job, my life. I am getting sick thinking about it all, and I don't know why I keep talking to myself in my head. I'm going to write some of it down. Maybe I should tell the doctor when I see him? Yes I will tell him. Maybe I am going bloody mad! Oh gosh, I do hope not!

***

Sitting in the doctor's surgery I feel shaky. I cannot stop twiddling with my hair and have been doing a lot of that lately. I stop. Someone coughs. I took up, it's an elderly man; he looks frail and his chest sounds full of phlegm. Poor man, I hope he's OK.

"Miss Sophie Taylor, please." Dr Grant's familiar voice calls me softly.

I stand, smile at him, and follow him into his room.

"Hello there, please sit, Miss Taylor, how can I help?"

"I'm just not feeling myself right now. I had a day off work this week, and I wasn't even sick. I never have a day off doctor. And ever since I have been struggling to get out of bed."

I stop and look at him, wanting him to say something.

"OK. And how long have you been feeling like this?"

"Oh just a few weeks, but I just seem to be getting worse and I don't know why"

"Worse? In what way?"

"Well, I can't seem to concentrate for long on anything. My brain feels like I'm taking *speed*; like I keep reading the same sentence in a book over and over, or terrible thoughts keep coming into my head, and going over and over"

"What kind of thoughts?"

"Oh, like I keep feeling sorry for everyone. I see a homeless man in the street and cannot stop thinking about him, I see old people and wish they were young again. I keep thinking I'm going to lose my job because I had the day off and I can't do my job as well at the moment..." I stop talking and look at Dr Grant; his soft facial lines, his kind eyes and his greying hair.

"How are you eating?" he asks.

"Erm, well, not very well. I keep forgetting to eat, or I can't be bothered"

"That's not so good is it?" he asks not waiting for an answer "and sleep, how are you sleeping?"

"Not very well, doctor, my brain is buzzing when I'm in bed. I do get to sleep but if I wake up I start thinking and worrying again"

"Worrying about what?"

"That I will lose my job, that I won't be able to pay my bills, that my family will come into ill health, all sorts of things"

"And do you believe those things will happen?"

"Well, no, not really, but then, yes, at the time I do. I don't know doctor, I'm confused"

"OK. And how is your social life – are you getting out and about with friends, family maybe?"

"I was"

"Was?" he raises his eyebrows a little and breaks into a small smile.

I cannot stop shuffling in my seat. It's like a bloody interview!

"Yes, was!" *OK that was a little abrupt, drop the attitude* Sophie "I mean I was until a few weeks ago. I was going to the gym, seeing my family, seeing friends, but now, well the last few weekends, I've stayed in. I just haven't felt like seeing anyone or being happy. I have enough trouble at work putting on that face"

"What a happy face?"

"Yes"

"OK, has anything happened lately that may have contributed to you feeling this way? Any sad events, or triggers?"

"Erm…" Crumbs, what has been happening? Think, Sophie, think!

Dr Grant is typing on his computer keyboard. It's a little distracting. *Is he even listening to me anymore anyway? Am I just boring? Wasting his time?*

"Anything come to mind?" he asks again.

"Oh er, no not that recently. My Aunt died last summer - that was very sad. But I'm over it now"

"Were you close?"

"Yes we were"

"Are you taking your Citalopram?"

"Yes, and it's been great for my depression doctor, it really has"

"It's possible, you know, for us to think we are over things when we aren't. Grief can take a long time to get over and sometimes if we push ourselves to get over it too quickly, it can pop up again down the line. I'm not saying that's what this is, it's just a thought, and sometimes pills are not enough; sometimes a talking therapy is beneficial. But what I am going to do is refer you to the mental health team for an assessment…"

"Mental health team! I'm not mad, am I doctor?"

He smiles. "No, Miss Taylor, I am not saying that at all. You will have an assessment, where you will be asked questions like I have today, and then they may refer you for some counselling, or another therapy, whichever they feel is best for you" I frowned. "It's nothing to worry about. It is possible you are still suffering with some symptoms of depression, and there are different ways in which our services can help, so that you can feel better again, back to yourself, OK?"

I nod.

He tells me I will receive a letter in the post, shortly, with an appointment, suggesting that it might take a couple of weeks or so before I see someone, and that they will report my progress back to him. So I will not necessarily have to see him again for this issue.

I thank him, my head bowed slightly and turn to leave, bumping into the door as I swing round.

"Ouch!" I shout.

"Oh, Miss Taylor, are you OK?"

"Yes, yes I'm fine" I say putting on a smile.

"OK, well, take it slowly and take care of yourself" he calls after me.

I shut the door, walk straight through the waiting room without looking at anyone and go home.

When I reach home I realise that I don't remember one bit of the journey from the doctor's *I must have got home on automatic, how odd.*

***

I have no plans for this weekend, it's Saturday morning, and I have decided to go to Victoria on the lookout for Malcolm. I sling on some jeans, a t-shirt, my thick cable knit cream jumper, my long, mustard timberland boots, my multi coloured scarf and my parker. Its bloody cold out and I plan on walking around outside today.

Just as I open the door, the phone starts ringing in the hall. I shut the door quick against the icy wind and answer the phone.

"Hello, Sophie here" *Oh I do sound fed up!*

"Darling! How are you? I haven't heard from you in two and half weeks! So glad you are OK, what have you been doing my love?"

"Oh, not much… working… you know, boring stuff"

"Oh dear that's not like you – haven't you seen your friends? What about Samantha, or Shelley? Have they not been round?"

"No" I sigh.

"OK, what's up darling, I can hear you are fed up, what's happened?" she says this in a condescending voice as if I've had a trauma over something stupid and it annoys me a little.

"Nothing, mum, nothing's happened; that's just the point!" I say abruptly; I just cannot help myself.

"Mmm, sounds like nothing" she snorts then she changes her tune "Come on, you can tell me, you know you can always talk to me"

I breathe heavily.

"Sorry mum, I've just not been feeling all that good as late, and I went to see the doctor today"

"Oh my, it's not something serious is it?" she questions.

"No mum, it's not. I've just been feeling a little low, that's all. The doctor says it might still be depression symptoms or something, and he's referred me to some counsellor or something, to help me out. He seems to think it has something to do with Nanna's death; like I've not grieved it properly"

"Oh" is all she says.

"Yeah well, I'm sure it's just a blip and I'll be feeling right as rain again soon"

"Yes, darling, I hope so. So, let's get together shall we? I've missed you."

"Yes mum, let's"

"How about tomorrow? I'm doing your favourite nut roast, how about you come over for lunch and we can have a good old chat?"

I pause. Then I say "Yes. That will be great – I look forward to it!"

"Oh marvellous darling! See you around twelve?"

"Yes, twelve it is"

"Good. Have a lovely day then, and see you tomorrow!" Mum sounds excited, and I feel loved and warm, and not just because I am wrapped up for the Antarctic standing in my hall.

"I will, you too. Love you"

"Love you too, bye"

"Bye"

As I put the phone down I get a slight surge of happiness fly through my body. *See, it's as easy as that* I tell myself. *I am a happy person; I'm just having a blip!*

I head out, the wind slapping me in the face with its bitterness and I realise that I have been sweating. It must have been the hall radiator. I'm cooling off quickly so I wrap my scarf around my neck once more round. I must look like I'm going up Mount Everest or something!

I get the train to Victoria and feel like I am 'on a mission' to find Malcolm. I don't even know what I will do if I do see him; just watch him, follow him, talk to him – who knows. I haven't got all that part planned out, I just feel a need to go look for him.

***

Malcolm woke early and decided upon a slow walk this morning to Hyde Park. So, he left the hustle bustle of Victoria station with its crowds of people with suitcases on wheels and weekend bags, coming and going to all sorts of places, and found himself on Grosvenor Place, where he passed a lovely looking Thai restaurant called the 'Mango Tree'. He glanced in through the large windows to see the neatly laid out tables and comfy chairs and remembered his last meal there; Tom Yum soup, Green chicken curry with jasmine rice and coconut rice with mango, washed down with a few Singha beers. His tummy rumbled as he could almost taste each course from his memory. It's a very good restaurant – fine dining no less. Someone bumped into him and he stumbled.

He heard a ladies voice say "Oh Sorry!" then as he turned round, the middle aged lady screwed her face into a grimace and walked on mumbling "disgusting!" under her breath. Malcolm watched her walk further and further away *She wouldn't have behaved like that to me if I'd just walked out of the that restaurant the last time; rudeness and disgust just because I look like a homeless person. What a shame!*

His stomach grumbling at him again jolted Malcolm out of his thoughts and he walked on, past the long wall on his right that spanned the length of the road and around the corner and sported a barbed wire and mesh canopy on top. It looked like a prison wall, noted Malcolm, but it wasn't; it was actually the *Buckingham Palace Gardens* wall. *Oh behind that wall lay wealth and royalty, servants and sophistication. Now, Queen Elizabeth* Malcolm pondered *she has a big job on her hands, born into royalty, made a Queen when young, and serving Great Britain and the Commonwealth as their Monarch ever since. She has to get up, go to events, coiffured and well dressed; an endless string of meeting the crowds that want to glimpse her unveiling of ships and statues, hospitals, places of industry… Oh yes, she has been a dedicated woman who has taken her responsibilities and duties as our Queen and executed them with grace and honour. When she agreed to serve her Country at her Coronation in 1953, she meant it.*

He crossed the huge, busy road, with ease. He was not frightened of the many red buses and cars that passed him as he ducked in front of or behind them to get to the other side. Reaching the wall, he turned the corner and headed towards the four pillars that stood at the top of Constitution Hill. He crossed the road and read the writing on the plaque in front of the pillars

A DEBT OF HONOUR
THE MEMORIAL GATES

This Memorial was inaugurated by Her Majesty, The
Queen during the Golden Jubilee Year, 2002.
It commemorates the service and sacrifices of five
million men and women from the Indian Sub-
continent, Africa and the Caribbean, who volunteered
to fight with the British in the two World Wars,
1914–1918 and 1939-1945.
This is the first time their magnificent contribution
has received fitting recognition.
With so many descendants of these volunteers now
living in the United Kingdom, the Memorial Gates
serve to remind us all of our shared sacrifices in times
of greatest need.

Malcolm read on, taking in the rest of the
details about how many volunteers were involved in
each war, and where they were from, such as the
Ghurkas and British African colonies.

There was a small enclosed area next to the plaque, where many people had laid poppy wreaths with messages. He read about the unveiling of this area all those years ago – it was an important Memorial.

As Malcolm headed towards Hyde Park, he realised how cold he was, shivering in fact. Being stirred up by the memorials and his thoughts of those millions who died in the two Great Wars, he'd forgotten it was spitting with rain, but he now felt it like a sheet of ice was slapping him in the face. He walked a little faster to warm up, and headed down into the Park Lane Subway, where it was much warmer and protected from the harsh wind. He began to doubt whether Robbie would turn up at the park, and felt stupid for even suggesting it, bearing in mind the weather conditions, so settled down in the subway for a while to warm up. He had some cardboard rolled up on the outside of his rucksack so laid that on the floor, pulled out his sleeping bag and pulled it round himself once he'd settled himself on the ground.

Within five minutes, someone had dropped a fifty pence piece on his sleeping bag and walked on, with no acknowledgement of what they had just done; their act of kindness towards a 'hobo'. It was a young lad, of around twenty five, dressed in jeans, grey trainers and a smart black jacket, and as Malcolm glanced after him, he noticed that the lad had earphones in his ears, the white lead from them leading into his right hand jacket pocket. *Ah music* mused Malcolm. He could do with listening to some Kaiser Chiefs or something like them right now; with the volume very high! *'Yes, I am a very long way away from home' Huh, well it's kind of true!*

Malcolm sat there for a good hour warming up and watching the world go by; men and women in a rush, friends or family chatting, people on their mobile phones, others with headphones in their ears, but many had one thing in common; they avoided eye contact with the man sitting on the floor on the cardboard warming himself inside his sleeping bag. *Oh to be so obviously here, yet so invisible* Malcolm thought, and he immediately pulled out his notebook and biro and wrote those words down.

He didn't meet up with Robbie until later in the afternoon. It's not like they had agreed on a time anyway; that didn't seem to be the 'done thing' with Robbie, who certainly insisted how much he liked his 'freedom' on the streets. It may have worked out that they didn't see each other at all for a few days; meetings were based upon coincidences and being in the same place at the same time.

He was wandering along Grosvenor Place when Malcolm caught sight of Robbie on the other side of the road, walking in the other direction.

"Oi mate!" he shouted over.

Robbie looked up and around but it took a few seconds for him to recognise Malcolm who was waving at him vigorously.

"Ah, Malcolm, how's it going?" he shouted back.

Malcolm didn't waste any time and crossed the road as quickly as he could, darting in between the cars and buses; two of which sounded their horns at him. "Yeah, yeah" he mumbled, pre-occupied with reaching the other side.

"Bloody hell mate, you wanna be a bit more careful!" said Robbie.

"Agh, so do they!" Malcolm replied, gesturing back towards the road.

Robbie smiled.

Malcolm patted Robbie on the shoulder as he walked up to him. "Wanna hang out?" he enquired.

"Yeah OK" Robbie agreed with a little pleasure in his voice; a slight smirk on his face.

I am not going to tell him too much he thought to himself *just a few things.*

"How about the park?" Robbie added.

"It's a bit bloody cold for that isn't it mate? Are you mad?"

"Well you might be, but the cold makes you feel alive doesn't it Malcolm?"

"Well yes I guess so; that is if you aren't completely numb with it!" he laughed.

"Right yeah, well just for a bit eh?"

Malcolm hesitated, moving from one foot to the other quickly whilst blowing out air from his mouth. It looked like smoke as it hit and flowed through the air. He capitulated.

"OK" he said looking directly into Robbie's eyes.

They smiled at each other briefly, and turned to head off to Hyde Park, up towards Marble Arch with its surrounding statues and huge busy roads.

They walked under the subway Malcolm had been warming himself in earlier, and he was now glad that he had, given that he was now going to all but freeze in the park and lose all his stored heat.

"I like chilling under here sometimes" said Robbie.

Malcolm laughed "Do you? Well, I like warming up under here!"

Robbie glanced at him, frowning like a child might when his father has just told everyone a lame joke; as in 'duh'

"It's good to laugh Robbie" said Malcolm, catching Robbie's expression out of the corner of his eye.

"Yes. Maybe." said Robbie, unenthusiastically.

"Look at those arseholes" came a loud male voice echoing down the subway "fucking lazy wankers" Robbie and Malcolm looked up to see a young lad of around twenty, whom the voice belonged to, walking towards them with five accomplices, friends, whatever they were.

"Yeah, lazy, and dirty bastards" scowled one of the other lads. They were all around the same age and with their swaggers, hoodies, and evil looking eyes; they looked like trouble.

Malcolm felt himself hold his breath, waiting for a punch in the face or something. Robbie just carried on as he was.

As the lads reached them, two of them shoved Robbie who was nearest to them, so that he stumbled.

"Yeah, you belong on the floor mate" snarled the first lad.

Robbie just coughed, regained himself and just carried on walking. He didn't seem perturbed. Malcolm had frozen for a split second, but breathed out slowly and quickly. He continued walking with Robbie once he realised that the lads just had big mouths and didn't seem to be planning on any violence, since they had carried on walking.

"Hey, were you scared there mate?" asked Malcolm.

"No, not really; all mouth and no trousers, those sorts"

"Do things like that happen often?"

"No, not really"

"Have you ever been hurt for living on the street?"

"Yep. I got smashed in by three guys once. They said I was the scum of the earth" Robbie told him without looking at him.

"YOU were scum of the earth! What about them? They were the scum!"

"Anyway, you should know Malcolm, what you've never had any shit for living on the streets before?"

Malcolm quickly answered "Yes. Yes, I have. Not for a while though. It just surprised me"

"Well then"

Malcolm made a mental note to stop saying stupid things.

Entering the park, the wind whipping round their ears, Malcolm asked Robbie where he fancied hanging out. Robbie suggested they head towards the lake, where they found quite a crowd of people with bags of bread and other bits of food they were feeding to the ducks, geese and swans. Adults cooed over their children, and kept them from getting too close to the birds, others were taking photos; many looked like tourists from various countries. Burqas, head-scarfs, woolly hats; all manner of clothing keeping people covered up and warm amidst the icy breeze skimming over the lake towards them.

Malcolm and Robbie walked past slowly, occasionally glancing at those they passed, mainly looking at the concrete floor on which they were treading, heads bowed.

"I need a drink" said Robbie.

"Oh yes, what type?" asked Malcolm, expecting that he meant something alcoholic.

"Water. There's a fountain down there"

"Oh"

A little further along, Robbie walked to the right to find the water fountain and bent to take some of it in. "Ouch, that's bloody cold!" he grimaced, his hand over his mouth.

"Sensitive teeth mate?"

"Yes" Robbie frowned and leaned over to take more water. "Have some" he added when he'd finished.

Malcolm had some, but soon needed to urinate.

"What do you do for a piss around here?" he asked.

Robbie screwed his face up. "Well, do what you usually do, piss over by those trees, but make sure there's no-one around. Why are you asking me?"

"Oh I don't know mate, I just haven't been in here before" he lied.

Robbie shook his head. "Well, I don't know where *you* go, but there are no lavatories for us, no matter where we are"

Malcolm disappeared for a few minutes and returned to the fountain to find Robbie sitting on a bench nearby. He sat next to him and Robbie turned to him and said "I've changed my mind; I don't want to talk about anything today"

Malcolm was disappointed, but could see from Robbie's face that he was serious and sure. "OK mate, no worries; maybe tomorrow eh?"

"Maybe" Robbie replied.

They sat silently for half hour or so, before deciding to go their separate ways.

***

I'm on my way home again now. It's just too cold to hang out any longer. I sat in *Pret A Manger*, wandered around, looked at a few shops in Victoria station where I bought a new scarf, but I didn't see Malcolm. I feel disappointed as I sit on this train, but then I am lucky to get a seat! It's busy. I stare at my lap, as many others do - a typical trait of tube users – and peer into the plastic carrier bag at my new scarf.

I shouldn't have bought that. I must take it back next week. Malcolm could do with a scarf much more than me. Or all the other homeless people living on the streets. Oh yes, I simply must take it back. I'm always buying things for myself. Still, I don't have any kids to spoil. I don't have a husband to spoil. So, it's only me. Even so, I have a scarf, so I don't need another one; it's not a necessity. From now on I am only going to buy things I really NEED!

I sigh much more loudly than I meant to, and as I look up, two women and a man standing in front of me, swaying with the train's movements, were staring at me, as if I had just insulted them or something. I look down again until I hear my stop coming up, then rise from my seat, and gently push past everyone with the polite and quiet "Excuse me" that I am used to saying on a regular basis in these circumstances.

After my second train journey, I walk my usual ten minute route through suburbia, and arrive at my front gate, which I open and close behind me. I walk up my short path to my front door, take my keys from my coat pocket, open the door and walk in, closing it behind me. It's strange, but I am noticing everything I am doing, every action, analysing every thought. It's like I am watching myself doing everything as if I am out of my body. Very strange.

I begin to eat the sandwich I picked up at the station earlier, pulling it out of its cardboard wrapping; falafel and salad. I find I have finished it but I cannot remember eating it. I have the faint taste of it in my mouth, but strangely that's the only recollection I have. I look at the time and it seems that I've been home two hours already, but feel like I just walked in the door. I sigh.

I pour myself a glass of water and go to bed to sleep, without brushing my teeth. I did think about doing it, as it's something I do every morning and every night, but I cannot be bothered, that is all.

In bed I feel comforted by the soft, thick duvet which I wrap around me tight, my head on my soft pillows, and I think of Malcolm; out there in the cold somewhere, along with so many others, with no bed to sleep on and no heating to keep him warm. And then I stop thinking…

***

Liz woke with her radio alarm, to the local station's 'Sunday morning hits' theme. She hit the slumber button to give herself nine more minutes with her eyes shut, and it turned on again, although she felt sure it had only been one minute as that's how it felt.

She stretched her arms in the air and let out a loud yawn, before throwing the covers back and jumping out of bed.

She performed ten minutes of yoga stretches, to ease the creaks from her slender body, then went downstairs to her little kitchen/lounge, filled the kettle with water and flicked the on switch.

Tea made, toast toasted, butter spread, she flopped onto her sofa and slurped and munched her way through breakfast. She didn't usually eat like that, but no-one could see her so why not she'd thought, although it didn't feel right without her usual dining etiquette.

Breakfast done, she had a quick shower, blow dried her long blonde hair, dressed in jeans, a t-shirt, a cardigan and black ankle boots, and headed off out the door to her car.

The drive to Thomas' house was quick, since there's little traffic early on a Sunday compared to most other times, so she'd only listened to a few songs on the radio 'I Will Survive' by Gloria Gaynor, 'Brown Girl In The Ring' by Boney M and her favourite 'Dancing Queen' by ABBA, to which she sang along loudly, plus a short news bulletin telling her about how the storms have devastated people's lives and homes. *Very sad* she thought, grimacing at the details. The weather report then told of more storms to come, faster winds, lots more rain… "Ooh, bleak" she said out loud, turning the radio off just before reaching Thomas' driveway.

He was waiting at the door smiling by the time she'd got out of her car "Hey sis'" he called.

"Hey brother" she replied laughing and they greeted each other with a tight hug and kiss on the cheek before heading indoors.

"Can we look at the photos again?" asked Liz with a big grin.

"OK, dear, anything for you" said Thomas with slight hesitation. He was simultaneously thinking *I knew you were going to say that, and I wish we didn't have to today.* It's not that Thomas doesn't care anymore for his brother, but sometimes he wants to think about him fondly, and other times, he would rather get on with life in the moment and feels that it's best not to live in the past. This was one of those days he felt the latter. But hey ho, he would keep smiling.

"So, has anything exciting been happening with you? At work? Any dates?" Liz was always interested in her brother's life and feelings, which he did share when he felt like it; *It's what men do* was his excuse for his inability to share emotions at times when they were at their peak.

"Not too much, Liz, just the usual"

"Mmm, sounds interesting!" Liz teased, knowing that this was his way of hiding something. "Well, maybe more about that later then, hey Thomas?"

"Ha, bloody ha" Thomas kept a straight face.

Liz ignored him. "Right well, for now, it's time for tea, hey what?"

"Quite right!"

"OK, I shall make it and you can go fetch the album"

"Right-e-o" Thomas walked out of the room, leaving Liz to make tea and look around the kitchen for any clues as to a possible new 'lady friend' of Thomas'. But, even her eagle eyes couldn't pick up on anything in particular.

"Here it is" Thomas presented the album and placed it on the kitchen table. When they sat down with their mugs of tea, Liz and Thomas both said simultaneously "Déjà vu" and laughed.

***

I wake up and almost wish I was going to work. I feel melancholy and could do with the company, but I told my friends I was busy with stuff this weekend, so it's my own fault. I reach for my mobile phone on the side table, to check the time, and notice there's a new

SMS waiting to be opened. I rub my eyes so I can focus on the name of the person who sent it but it's not a number from my contacts, so I just open the text, and then I wake up – very quickly!

Hello Miss Taylor, it's Mr Banks here from work. I wondered if you could meet for a coffee this afternoon?

"Oh my gosh" I say slowly, out loud, and then I begin to wonder what on earth he could want. *Does he want to sack me today, so I don't have to even go in tomorrow? Does he want to...* Well, actually I cannot think of any other reasons but that one, so my hands holding the phone begin to shake and I throw the phone onto the bed and sink under the duvet into the darkness for a few seconds. *No, Sophie, you cannot hide, you will have to face this. Be brave. Oh no, I cannot be brave, what about my rent? And my bills?* I begin to cry.

My phone vibrates on the bed. *Oh no, what now?*

I pick up the phone and frantically press the buttons to read the text, and get the wrong buttons in my haste, so I slow myself down and get it right eventually.

It's another text from the same number. *Miss Taylor, I'm so sorry to bother you on a Sunday, but it is important* ☺

A smiley face? That's odd. What is it, an "I'm going to sack you but I will smile while I am doing it" smiley face?

Oh god, I'll have to answer it, he sounds serious. So I carefully press the letters to form a reply.

OK, Mr Banks; that will be fine.

Send...

Within one minute, I receive a reply.

Good! How about the coffee house in front of the church in Maidenhead, say, 2.30?

Yes, that will be fine. I will see you there.

I throw the phone down so that it bounces on the duvet onto the floor, and without picking it up I head into the bathroom, where I look at myself in the mirror for around five minutes. *Checked up on where*

I live has he? Oh my gosh! I look tired. I look sad, I'd say. I smile but it's a weak smile, so I get on with brushing my teeth and take a shower before I cannot be bothered to do so.

Two cups of tea, a coffee, two bananas and a load of Sunday TV later, and I head out into the fresh, breezy air to begin the arduous journey to the coffee shop. I say arduous; it's not a difficult walk, just arduous in my mind, which is by now almost spinning.

But, when I open the door to the coffee shop and blow in with the wind I catch sight of Mr Banks, and I smile. I smile because he is smiling at me and he suddenly looks quite gorgeous with his short dark hair, his lit up eyes and his cosy cable knit beige jumper. I feel almost embarrassed when go over and say hello to him, due to my inner thoughts – I almost want to kiss him. He says hello back and gets up from his chair to greet me, pulling my chair out for me. *Ooh he's being a proper gentleman before he rips the soul from me eh!*

"So glad you could come, Sophie. Can I get you something to drink? Tea? Coffee?" *Oh his smooth voice is delicious, and he's so well spoken...*

"A cappuccino please"

"Anything to eat? They do some mean cakes in here so I've heard"

"Oh, no thanks, just the coffee"

Even if I was hungry I wouldn't eat anything now – my stomach is tied up in knots and it's now fluttering because as Mr Banks turned towards the counter, I got a good look at his pert looking bottom in his smart, dark blue jeans. And those shoes, very nice brogues. I glance towards his seat and look under the table, but I cannot see any paperwork; not even a bag. I would expect him to have some sort of papers for me to sign or a letter or something…

"Here we go" he says putting two mugs down on the table. "Uno cappuccino!"

I wonder why he's so bloody jolly?

"Thank you"

"So" he began "have you been up to much this weekend so far?"

"Erm, well no, not a lot. I went into town yesterday for a bit, but, well, can I just ask you why you asked me to come for a coffee, I'm not feeling very good about it"

"Oh, yes, sorry, I expect you thought it was something to do with work didn't you?"

"Well, yes, of course"

"No, no it's nothing to do with work actually. Now, Sophie, this is going to sound very unprofessional, and I shouldn't be doing this but… how can I put this… well, Sophie, I like you and just wanted to meet up today to see you on a more casual basis"

"Oh" I cannot find anymore words to say.

"I know, it's so wrong, but I was rather hoping that you might come out for dinner with me?"

"Dinner? What do you mean, like a kind of date or something?"

"Well, yes, yes that's exactly what I mean"

"Oh my gosh"

He looks at me expectantly, with wide eyes, but his face soon drops.

"I've crossed the line, I know. I'm sorry, I shouldn't have asked. I don't know what came over me. I am sorry I asked."

"No, no, don't be sorry. I'm honoured you'd ask me. And… I am going to say… yes" I laugh and let out air through my mouth that I have been partially holding in for far too long, in a soft sigh of relief.

"Oh, brilliant! Just brilliant!"

***

Malcolm woke up and his whole body ached. He decided to get up straight away before the cold set in and he finds he cannot move at all. *Get walking and warm up.*

He trampled the streets, meeting a few other homeless people and a couple of beggars who have a home, but beg on the street for their beer or drug money. They all looked like they were on the way to somewhere. *The way to where?* He pondered. *Where is there to go? There is no final destination.* He'd been up writing in his notebook in the light of a shop the night before, so he was feeling philosophical, but he didn't share any of his enlightenments with any fellow beggars. They were an interesting bunch though and some he'd seen quite a few times before. He found that the longer he was around, the more they would be willing to share a few words. It was definitely a community, the homeless of London, and it could be cliquey, but he was slowly making progress into their group. And he did want *in*.

He was just watching the news on TV through a shop window, about all the terrible storms lashing through the UK, especially in Devon and Somerset areas, when he felt a tap on his shoulder. He turned to see Robbie pulling a slightly clownish face at him.

"Alright mate?" asked Malcolm.

"Yes, I'm alright. Better than yesterday"

"Good. Have you seen all this? Storms and flooding all over western England?"

"No, but then we've got enough rain here to worry about"

"It's true, but what about the poor bastards down there? I wouldn't fancy kipping in a shop doorway down that way!"

"Right" Robbie said in a *matter of fact* manner, and looked at the floor.

"It's bloody awful" carried on Malcolm "Just awful"

"So, why are you so bothered?" asked Robbie accusingly.

"Just got me thinking, that's all"

"Oh you don't want to do too much of that, old chap, that could be dangerous" Robbie wasn't joking, but was taken aback even more than Malcolm by his own voice; the voice of his past. He'd tried to shake it off but sometimes it came back at odd times.

"Well brought up, weren't you?" Malcolm asked.

"Yes. I guess so." Robbie said quietly.

"Want to have a chat today?"

"Yes"

"Good. Let's go… to the park I assume"

"Yes"

Walking past the 'Mango Tree' on Grosvenor Place, Robbie told Malcolm that he had taken his wife there twice. Malcolm didn't comment.

In the park, sat on a bench, Robbie told Malcolm more about himself and his family. His daughter, Francine, had loved the colour lilac, Barbie dolls and her favourite food was chocolate, his son, Timothy wanted to be a chef like his dad, and was always watching him cook in the kitchen at home and his son, James, loved cars and trains, and wanted to be a formula one driver. Robbie spoke of his family with much love and a sparkle in his eyes, so Malcolm asked him if he'd ever tried to see them again since he left, to which Robbie firmly replied "No".

"Why not?"

"What looking like this? Are you mad? They wouldn't want a father like this!"

"Well… it might be better than having no father at all, mightn't it? What about if your wife has a man; that man will be filling your role?"

Robbie stared at the floor. He looked solemn again, but said nothing.

After a few moments Robbie concluded "This is where I belong; in the gutter. Like my wife said"

"Did she really?"

"Well, no, but she ended up being more interested in the money, than my feelings, so I assume…"

"Oh assume. Assumptions are often wrong you know" butted in Malcolm.

"Maybe… I just don't know. I haven't thought about it for a long time; brushed it off because it hurt too much. I miss my kids though Malcolm. I have missed them every day, think about them every day and I send my love every day to them, in my mind…" He wiped the back of his hand over his moistened eyes and tailed off.

Malcolm patted him on the back and said nothing for a while.

Eventually, he asked Robbie to tell him more about his time as a chef. It turned out Robbie was a pot washer at first in a small hotel restaurant, and he did this for two years, until his interest in cooking became so intense at work, that they gave him a trial kitchen assistant role, just to prepare vegetables, wash salad items and other preparation tasks. But, he showed such flare, that when a Commis chef position came up, they offered it to him, which he snapped up quickly, eventually moving on to the position of Chef de Partie. He loved it, cooking steaks, *Duck a l'orange* and other traditional fayre. The extra money from his promotion allowed him to move out of his bedsit into a small flat. It wasn't the space he was bothered about; it was the fact that he finally had a kitchen, albeit limited. He could then practise cooking all sorts of food and bought cookery books written by the likes of the Roux brothers.

His passion for cooking grew and he began to design new recipes for the hotel, which went down very well, bar the head chef, who was a little peeved at his menus being snubbed for his junior chef's offerings. It didn't take long before the head chef left, and Robbie became head chef himself.

The restaurant thrived, and gained many new local customers and repeats, as well as great feedback, and within six months he was talent spotted by a successful, fine dining restaurant owner. Although he wouldn't be head chef, he'd be Sous-Chef, he would learn and earn a lot more, so he took the jump.

"To cut a long story short, Malcolm, I became so hot at my job, I decided to start my own restaurant two years later, using the money I'd saved since I was sixteen and some I'd inherited."

"Oh, so who passed away?"

"I might tell you that some other time. But back to the restaurant, I opened a very smart place, all the waiters had a uniform, I did a la carte fine dining, got to know the ropes, and won some young chef awards. And by the time I was twenty four, I had earned the best award ever – a Michelin star" He stopped and looked up to the sky almost in awe of his past.

"So… you were a brilliant chef. What happened?"

"Well, I married my girlfriend, had three children, earned a small fortune, and then she decided she didn't want to know me anymore."

"What? Really? Just like that? That simple?"

"I was drinking; a lot. I hit her, a couple of times. I regret it, I said sorry, but sorry wasn't enough. I drank more, I took some drugs, and I worked hard. She said I didn't care about her or the kids anymore and she filed for divorce, I had to move out and find some rented bloody apartment and then, icing on the cake, she stopped me from seeing my own kids – said I wasn't fit to look after them on my own. So, we were down to supervised visits. I drank more and so it went on." He started laughing.

"Erm, mate, why are you laughing, it's not funny"

"Exactly, but if you don't laugh Malcolm you go mad. Bit late for me now, but at least I can laugh about myself eh? I lost the restaurant within five months. I fucked it all up. I couldn't work anymore, only drink and spend my money on cocaine"

"Oh mate, that's sad"

***

I'm on my way home from the coffee shop. We were there for nearly two hours and we laughed a lot, chatted a lot and I think I fell in love. I feel like I am on a high; like I've taken some 'happy drug' that has transformed my mood from extremely low to extremely high. I feel like dancing down the aisle of this bus. Perhaps I should have walked home; burnt my excitement off. My heart feels like it will burst. Mr Banks, fancy that! It may well be wrong to date my boss, but hey I couldn't say no.

    He has no children, is totally single, he is fit due to his love of tennis (I doubt I'll be joining him there, but then he likes to train with his mates), he loves films, documentaries, reading, cooking and although he first asked me to go out for a meal, I suggested that maybe he would like to show off his culinary skills to me and he said yes straight away!

I laugh out loud, and a woman on the seat opposite glances my way and smiles "Nice to hear someone happy love"

I giggle "I agree"

Oh please let him be the one! I can't believe I thought he was going to sack me and turns up wanting a date!

***

It's Monday morning. Despite being tired, due to the excitement of my forthcoming date stopping me from sleeping well last night, I feel on top of the world. I got into work early and am buzzing around, sorting out customer queries, letters and emails. I haven't seen him yet, but hope he's in today.

"Did you have a nice weekend Sophie?" asks Janice, my friendly assistant.

"Yes I did, thank you Janice, how about you?"

"Yeah it was OK, a bit boring but I went to see 'Railway Man' at the cinema and that was brilliant!"

"Oh, is that the guy who was working on the Burma railway?"

"Yes, and he was tortured and all sorts – Colin Firth is such a brilliant actor too"

"I might have to see that sometime Janice, I love films based on true events"

"I would. I can highly recommend it"

"Good. So, how's the situation with Mrs Briggs, have her issues been resolved?" I ask, checking through the rest of my emails.

"Oh yes, after the whole of last week complaining, she finally…"

I cannot hear her anymore as a new email has pinged into my inbox and it's from Mr Banks *Can you come and see me in my office asap please?*

Instead of the dread I felt yesterday morning when he asked me to meet with him, I feel like jumping up and racing straight in there, but I won't. So I wait - just two minutes I wait. In the meantime I ask Janice to repeat what she has said about Mrs Briggs, to keep me occupied, and then wander over to knock on his office door.

"Come in" he shouts.

As I enter, his face turns from serious into a big smile immediately, and I say "Hello Mr Banks"

"Oh Sophie, please don't call me that anymore, please use my name"

"Oh no, I think it best to keep things the same in work don't you?"

He pauses momentarily then agreed "Yes, maybe you are right. Anyway, I was just wondering if you would like to sample my cuisine tonight? That is, if you are not too busy?" he beams.

I cannot stop smiling, and say "Yes, that would be great"

"OK, I shall come and pick you up, say around seven?"

"Erm, OK that will be great"

"Lovely, well jot your address down and I will see you at seven" he says passing me a note pad and Mont Blanc pen.

I write my address on the pad, bid him a good day and leave.

***

Seven o'clock on the dot, he picks me up in his black Mercedes Benz sports car, and we chat easily all the way to his house, which turns out to be a lovely detached, four bedroom house in Marlow of all places. Wow!

He opens the car door for me, and gets me a drink as soon as we get inside, after taking my coat and hanging it up.. Very gentlemanly I note.

Just as we say 'cheers', clinking our wine glasses together, the doorbell rings and he stops in his tracks and frowns. "Who's that?" he says.

"Well, there's only one way to find out" I muse.

"Excuse me" he says leaving the lounge. I can hear a mumbled conversation, including a female voice. I cannot hear what they are saying, but I don't have to wait long to find out who it belongs to as he comes back in with a blonde, tall lady.

"Sophie, sorry, this is my sister, Liz"

"Oh don't be sorry, it's lovely to meet you Liz" I say walking up to her to shake her hand.

"Lovely to meet you too" She beams and takes my hand warmly. "Thomas didn't tell me he had a lady friend"

"Well, my sister has just come to pick something up" interrupts Thomas "Here it is" he tells her, passing her what looks like a large photo album.

"Oh well, I know when I am not wanted" she laughs.

"You know I…"

"No, don't worry Thomas, I completely understand. Lovely to meet you Sophie; I hope to see you again"

***

Malcolm woke Tuesday morning with a jolt. He looked up to see a policewoman above him saying "Wake up please, you must move on, you cannot stay there"

He was in a shop doorway and the shop was due to open in an hour – he hadn't realised. He mumbled something about not getting any peace, and sat up.

"Well, you know you cannot sleep in these public areas – we have to move you on"

"Yeah, yeah" Malcolm pulled himself out of his sleeping bag, quickly threw everything together and in or attached to his rucksack, and stumbled to his feet, all the time watched by the police woman. "I'm going!"

He wandered along the street for a short time, until he saw a guy with bright patterned trousers and a long sleeved top walking in his direction. The reason he noticed him is because he was so bright and chatty. He wasn't chatting to anyone, just himself, but so happy. "Alright chap?" he beamed at Malcolm as he got closer.

"Hi" Malcolm replied slight startled, but he stopped in his tracks to greet him.

"Good, good" the man was almost jumping from foot to foot, a big grin on his face. "Must go" he continued and then he raced off down the road.

Malcolm had seen him before; he was clearly a man of the streets and clearly using some sort of 'upper' but Malcolm had never actually had a conversation with him as he was always in a rush. *Maybe one day soon* He thought. And he wished the man would get hold of a coat as it was too cold to be going around without one like that.

He also thought about all the people he'd met so far on the streets as he wandered, sat down on the pavement, and asked passers' by for spare change quietly. He also thought about the possible choices homeless make about how they live their lives. He knew of various help centres, possible benefits, and hostels that take in the homeless to help them out. He would have to look into that; not just for his own means, but for Robbie and maybe other acquaintances of the streets of London.

"Come on mate" said a stern voice from above Malcolm, who was still sat on the kerb, where he'd been for two hours.

Malcolm didn't need to look up as he could tell it was a policeman by his dark boots and trousers. He looked up all the same, at a well-built copper with what seemed like not much hair and a rounded face.

"What's your name?" he asked.

"Malcolm"

"Well, Malcolm, you need to move along mate, you can't sit on the kerb like that. What if you got run over by a car eh?"

"Erm… Well, maybe I'd end up in hospital, with nice food, a comfy bed, a warm room, and nice nurses to look after me" Malcolm kept a straight face, but the policeman's face cracked into a smile and he laughed.

"Well, you've got a point there, but maybe you wouldn't like the pain you'd be in at the same time"

"Yeah well, you've got a point"

"OK, well, can you get up please and move along?"

"Yes, I sure will officer"

Malcolm got to his feet quickly and nearly fell over, as his legs had half 'gone to sleep' due to the amount of time and his position whilst sitting on the concrete floor.

"Easy!" said the policeman lending Malcolm a hand. "Have you been drinking?"

"Nope. I just got up too quickly"

"OK, fine"

Malcolm found the copper to be around his height (five foot ten) and as he studied his face, noticed his amazingly long and curly eyelashes framing his bright blue eyes.

I wonder what goes on behind those eyes thought Malcolm as he wandered off bidding the policeman farewell.

The policeman, Andy, stood for a moment and watched Malcolm wander aimlessly down the street, amongst the crowds, and he wondered what on earth brought Malcolm to become a man of the streets. He knew a few stories behind various street people, but not this one.

He decided to have a quick coffee in *Pret a Manger*, ready for the rest of the day's work. As he sat sipping his *flat white*, he thought about Malcolm and the possible backgrounds he may have come from, based upon his voice and demeanour, but soon reminded himself that a person's accent, poise, or level of intelligence only reflected a few things from a person's background, like where they were from, whether they went to school or university, whether they came from a poor or wealthy family. But, even then, it wasn't exact. It was guess work, complete guess work, until the real story came out from the individual.

Jen, his wife, had often told him about her clients too, so he was well informed about the vast differences between people, adversities they may come across and how they deal with those adversities. Jen was a drug therapy counsellor in a male prison up until two years before, when she decided to quit after having their second child, a little girl called Lucy. Their first born was a son, Lucas, who'd arrived just three years before Lucy. Having put him in day care while she pursued her career, she had decided she didn't want to do the same for her daughter, as those three years she'd taken Lucas to nursery had been tough – she'd felt extremely guilty at being selfish about her own needs.

Andy had agreed that they could live on his income, and she had promptly said goodbye to her job twelve weeks before Lucy was even born.

But, while she'd worked, she'd brought home stories of battered childhoods, sexual abuse, bullying, alcoholic fathers, and so much more, as the backgrounds of prisoners who'd ended up on drugs or alcohol, involved in robbery and mugging sprees came out. She never told him names or anything like that, as it was confidential, but Andy made up a name for each person he heard about. He had to visualise, had to really think about the individual guys, and how they might be feeling.

Empathetic is what you'd call Andy to sum him up. However, he was empathetic to other people, and not always to those closest to him.

He found himself jolted out of his thoughts, as a lady said loudly "Can I take this chair?" pulling at the chair opposite him.

He glanced up and told her she could.

He sipped his coffee, which was cooling fast, and thought about some of the *poor buggers out there on the streets...* like Mary, the woman who'd become an alcoholic due to depression and lost everything including access to see her own kids. She was about forty eight now and was part of the London street community, so she was never alone, but part of being that community, especially those who squatted, drugs and alcohol came at a high price and sexual abuse and rape were not uncommon partly because the women were outnumbered by the men and partly because some men in this world are bastards. Andy hated all crime, but his biggest hates were the harm of children and women by men; the strong picking on the weak like the cowards they were.

He knew an ex stockbroker, Liam, who'd been diagnosed bipolar, drank and gambled his money away, despite his wife and two children living with him, and who had left him once he'd gotten himself into real trouble with money. Due, mostly, to not taking his medications properly, all this had begun and come to a head in just two years. He had been out of control; his changing moods, of manic highs and desperate lows, had also made him unbearable to live with, and his wife might have been better off getting him help, but she'd had too much else on her mind, looking after her young sons and trying to keep the bills paid, that she'd simply not thought of it as a viable option. Who knows what she's doing now, but for sure, her estranged husband was out there somewhere on this cold night, living rough and out of control. He knew this as he'd not heard of him being arrested lately. Liam had been in and out of the police cells and prison, for disturbing the peace, petty theft, resisting arrest, and trespass and was well known to most of Andy's partners at work, so word would get around about the latest goings on of Liam.

Liam was another one who didn't want to know about any help on offer for the homeless, but Andy did know of quite a few who'd successfully taken advice from their local homeless centres, got themselves benefits, cleaned up, taken any shelter they were offered and had got themselves back on their feet and into a proper home again; many of whom had gone on to get jobs and become more stable. But, it wasn't just the desire to get the help that was required; there just were not anywhere near enough beds to house everyone overnight, there was not enough food in food banks to offer everyone, and it often depended upon the individual's ability to read and write, so some did shy away from forms and help out of pure pride sometimes. It was unusual the things people could be proud about, or not proud about, thought Andy.

Thinking too much and empathising too much were Andy's biggest problems. He commuted into work by train, thirty nine miles per day, five days per week, if not more, to do his job for the Metropolitan Police. He had a three bedroom semi-detached home which housed himself, his wife and two children, for whom he was now sole breadwinner, and he was feeling the pressure of that responsibility. He and his wife bickered a lot, she telling him all the time that he has no time for the children and doesn't even want to make time, which hurt him. She had decided nine months before that she was off sex until further notice and he had given up asking her when she thought she might like to try it again. And there was stuff from his past that he was not willing to face – yet.

Because of all these conflicting goings on, and the job now getting to him more and more as he witnessed death, murder, abuse or general crime on a daily basis, he found it hard to turn off work mode and step into relax mode at home. Wrongdoings by others were stuck in his brain, as he went over and over them, trying to find some peace.

So, it was no wonder, really, that he was in therapy. It wasn't just counselling therapy, and not one to one; this was psychotherapy – analytical group therapy to be precise.

He went once a week for one and half hours and had been in the group for ten months by now. His wife, Jen, supported him with going to the group, and she hoped that she would see some positive results soon, particularly in bringing out his pent up anger. She also wanted him to realise that he should spend more time focussed on his family, rather than just being present, which, in her mind, was all he did when he was at home. As far as she was concerned he was very good at DIY and a little over keen to do jobs around the house, or watch TV, than to engage in rest and play as a family group.

But what about Malcolm? What was he doing on the streets? Had he lost his job? His home? His wife? Had he been involved in drugs? Alcohol? Had he once been successful? What about his family? Andy conjured up many scenarios in his head of Malcolm being the boss of a big company, telling everyone what to do, or living in a big house, or living in a small house… he pictured a small semi, with its drive on the front, and tiny rectangle garden at the back, overlooked by the neighbours, who were very nosey and liked to peer… *Brr Brr Brr Brr*

"Oh shit!" said Andy out loud, as he was jolted from his day dream. "Bloody phone!"

He looked at the screen to see who it was and a small picture of his blonde wife was highlighted as it continued to vibrate. He placed the phone on the table, after checking the time, picked up his mug, swigged the last drop of cold coffee, wiped his mouth with a serviette, stood up and walked out of the coffee shop. As he closed the door behind him, he stood taller, brushed his blue uniform down and walked off, now back in Police mode.

***

Thomas was totally expecting the call, so it didn't surprise him at 7.15am the next morning, when his sister's number came up on his phone, as the Star Wars theme tune rang from its tiny speaker. He pressed the screen to receive the call.

"Hello Liz, good morning to you!" he exclaimed.

"Yes indeed, good morning dear brother. Did you have a good time last night?"

"Yes thank you, did you?"

"Ha! You know I only went home, but you… you had a date! And I want to know all about her"

"Well, dear sister, you will have to wait. There's not much to tell at the moment" he lied.

"Mmm, well I'm excited for you and I'd love to know who she is at least; can I come round tonight, around six? I won't stay long, I promise"

Thomas paused "Well, you could, but… oh no, it'll be fine, I'll see you about six. I much dash, I need to be in early today. Have a good one!"

"OK darling, you have a good one too, see you later!" Liz smiled.

***

I slept like a log. I feel so refreshed now, I cannot believe it. Maybe a bit of fun was what I needed, and well, a bit of man. I cannot stop smiling and I've only been awake for ten minutes. It makes a change to smile in the morning; I usually scowl at the alarm clock and hit the snooze button. Oh well, today is different.

I feed Bruno, my cat, and give him a cuddle, make coffee and get in the shower for a quick pick me up wash. As the cool water soaks my body, stimulating every part of my being, I let out a giggle as I think about those beautiful, sultry kisses we shared last night. Thomas is a dream. He's gentle, vigorous and sexy, all in the right quantities and I cannot wait to experience some more of his talents. He even loves cats, which is very important.

There's just one problem; he's still my boss. *Awkward. Shall I go in and ignore him, so no-one catches on? Shall I go and see him in his office and ask him what I should do? Shall I send him an email? Or should I just stop worrying about it and try to behave as I normally do? No, I simply cannot do that, not after last night. Oh my! I'm in a bit of a pickle now. Why does something so lovely have to be tinged with guilt and secrecy? Or does it? Maybe it doesn't.*

I've managed to wash my body and hair without even remembering I've done it, so I turn off the water and step out, reaching for one of my pink fluffy towels. *Mmm, I wonder if he likes pink? Or will I have to ditch all my girly stuff for him? Oh my gosh, stop it Sophie, he's not moving in… yet!* I giggle again.

When I enter the office, everyone is staring at me. Well, actually no-one is staring at me, but I had actually got myself into a bit of a state on the train imagining everyone would know, and would think it was wrong; I was wrong. I cannot speak though, so omit my usual greetings to everyone between the door and my desk. Janice has a day off, so I sit alone. Marilyn comes over.

"Hi Sophie how are you? You're not your bubbly self today, is everything OK?"

"Oh, erm, yes, yes, everything is fine" I say unable to keep eye contact with her. I pretend to look for something in my bag.

"Are you sure, lovey? You look a little distracted"

I look up at her and see that she is smiling kindly. She doesn't know. I look round and everyone is getting on with their stuff as usual and I breathe out heavily.

"That's the way lovey, you take some deep breaths"

I laugh. I feel so relieved. "Thanks Marilyn, I was just a little stressed from the train ride"

"Anything you want to share?"

"Oh no, not that interesting, just someone… well you know, the trains get more crowded every day it seems"

"Mmm, it must be hard commuting that far every day. Well, have a great day Sophie, and you know where I am if you need me." Marilyn soothed.

"Thanks Marilyn, I appreciate it."

She wanders back to her desk and I glance over to Thomas' office. The door is shut. I decide to get on with my day and do nothing with regard to him. *I shall let him make the first move!*

***

Thomas could just about see Sophie as he wandered across his office to a filing cabinet. He didn't want anything in the cabinet; he was just pretending, so he could check out what Sophie was doing. *She's typing at her desk, she looks busy. Shall I ask her to come in? Shall I email her? Shall I catch her at the end of the day? What if I miss her? I could text her… Yes, I'll text her.* He retreated back to his desk, picked up his phone and wrote a message *Hi Sophie, thanks for a lovely night last night! You look lovely today; may I say gorgeous… Want to do it again tomorrow?* He pressed send and wandered back over to the filing cabinet…

***

I can hear my phone vibrating in my bag. We are not supposed to answer calls in the office, but this is a text, and I simply cannot wait to read it, so I grab my phone and check it under the table. It's a text from Thomas… *Ooh, how lovely - tomorrow. Should I accept? I wonder what he's doing tonight? Maybe he's going out? Maybe he doesn't' want to appear too keen? Maybe I shouldn't appear too keen. Mmm, what to do?*

I decide not to answer straight away. Let him stew a little. So I place my phone back in my bag and carry on with my work.

***

She's just looked at her phone, my message says it's been received, yet she's not answering. I wonder why? Maybe she doesn't like me as much as I like her? Maybe she's busy? No, if she was busy, she'd say so, wouldn't she? Oh I know, maybe she needs to check her diary before she commits? I'll carry on with my work and see what happens... Thomas sat down at his desk.

***

OK, I've waited half hour, and cannot wait anymore. I also cannot play hard to get. Why would I want to blow out tomorrow? It would be like cutting off my nose to spite my face. And who said that the whole playing hard to get thing works with everyone anyway. He's keen, I'm keen, so let's do it. I type out a short text message in reply to his, accepting his offer, and finish it with three kisses. Phew, glad I've got that all clear in my mind now!

***

Yes! She's said yes. Now that's something to look forward to! Thomas was very pleased with this news.

***

"Just wondering where you were mate" Malcolm said, patting Robbie heavily on the back.

Jumping back, Robbie seemed perturbed at this gesture; at least his face said so.

"What the fu… oh, it's you!" he said miserably.

"Oh sorry I didn't know I was that bad" Malcolm offered, smiling a little, but not too much.

Robbie stared at Malcolm momentarily, and Malcolm stepped back, holding his hands up.

"OK, sorry mate, I didn't mean to…"

"It's fine. It's done."

Oh my, Robbie's very abrupt today thought Malcolm, planning his next move.

"So, Robbie, what you been up to?"

"Been at the hostel"

"Hostel? Which one?"

"Sallyander House"

"Not heard of that one, where is it?"

"Near Victoria"

"Any good?"

"It's a bed and it's warmer than being out here"

"Are you staying there tonight?"

"No idea. I'll queue up later and find out"

"Mind if I come with you?"

"No, be my guest. But I'll go first in the queue… just in case"

"Right; no problem"

"Well, I can't stand here all day" Robbie smirked cheekily, turning to leave.

"Eh? No, that's right, nor can I – things to do and all that"

"You coming then?" Robbie said abruptly, without turning round.

"Yes. I'm coming" Malcolm followed his friend. "Shall we get some tea?"

"Tea? What with?"

"This" Malcolm pulled out some coins from his pocket; an act which immediately had an effect on Robbie's face – from a down turned mouth, to a broad smile, from narrow, almost blank eyes, to almost sparkling, wide eyes.

"Simple things" Malcolm muttered, pleased with the effect his few pence could have on a person.

Getting the tea was not as easy as it sounds. Well, it was easy, it's just that…

Even in MacDonald's people stared. And some kids were holding their noses and giggling "Phew, stink!" and such like. *You have to be tough* Malcolm thought to himself *to survive*. He got the tea though, which they drank outside the entrance; steam pouring from the paper cup into the cold air. Both men savoured the heat, the taste and the wetness.

A few hours later, Robbie told Malcolm that they had better head over to the hostel, as the queues would start soon. "It doesn't really make any difference if we are standing here or there, but its better we are there, as it gets busy!"

"No doubt"

"Have you been to a hostel before?" Robbie asked, on the way there.

"No, not yet"

"How long have you been on the streets then, really?"

"Oh, um, about six months" Malcolm lied.

"Oh"

Robbie was right; the queue was almost as long as they were when *E.T.* came out at the cinema. So many desperate, homeless... men.

"Don't women come to these places?" Malcolm wanted to know.

"They go somewhere, but not here, this one's for men only"

"Oh. I see"

"Well, there are more men than women on the streets, aren't there? And the women have different privacy to guys"

"Yes. That's right" Malcolm's voice became quiet as he pondered this information. He would like to find out the ratio of women to men on the streets, or homeless, let's say.

He was shaken from his deep thoughts when Robbie nudged him to enter the hostel. He'd been thinking so hard, he hadn't even noticed that he had been shuffling along the queue as the men in front were allowed into the front doors of the hostel, and it was now his turn to 'check in'.

He was asked if he had any alcohol or drugs on him, his bag and body was searched, he was given a cup of water, and was told where to go. Robbie had waited for him, so they went to their dormitory together. Many beds greeted them as they entered a large room. Beds in the walls almost, like bunk beds, with a little curtain running along to offer complete privacy from the rest of the dorm. That is privacy from sight not noise; and it was noisy.

He'd been told that he could sleep the night, would have tea in the morning in the communal area and then he would check out at 9am sharp. No-one was allowed to stay in the hostel during the day; it was strictly open at 4pm and closed at 9am. Malcolm thought about all the staff in the daytime who would be clearing up after the barrage of men left, getting everything ready for the next lot to arrive. A bit like a hotel, but the guests were all male and all in need of a good wash. "What a job!" he mused out loud.

"Eh?" Robbie thought he was talking to him.

"Oh nothing, just thinking about something that's all"

"You're not thinking about getting a job are you?" Robbie studied Malcolm's face intently.

"No! Ha, that's a laugh!" Malcolm waved his hand like he was batting away a fly, and got on with inspecting his bed for the night.

***

"So, come on then, I want to know all about Sophie" Liz bubbled as her brother opened his front door to her. She walked straight past him, and into the kitchen, filled the kettle with water and turned to see him in the doorway, a little bemused. "Well?" she laughed, knowing how much her brother just wanted to ignore her question, change the subject, and see his sister leave without further inquisition.

"Oh! Why do you have to do this?" Thomas sighed.

"Because I'm your sister and I love you and want to know all about your happy bits"

"Happy bits?"

"Yes, happy bits!" she almost snapped "Now come on, spill the beans"

"Beans?" Thomas decided he wouldn't beat around the bush; it would be best to give Liz what she wanted, because she would get it somehow anyway – she can be very pushy when it comes to things like this. "Right, beans it is… Her name is Sophie as you know, she lives in Maidenhead and she is one of my employees"

"Em-ploy-ees?" Liz started.

"Yes, yes, an em-ploy-ee!" Thomas confirmed.

"Oh. Well, that's interesting" Liz smirked.

"Is it?" Thomas could use many words to describe it, but Sophie being his employee was not, in his mind, interesting; it was a problem. It was exciting as well, granted, but essentially it was a problem that couldn't be solved as easily as his daily crossword puzzles on the train.

It was also a problem that he didn't fancy tackling with his sister at that time, so, after telling her a few more details about Sophie and their first date, he told Liz he had some work to do on his computer, and she took the hint and left – all amicably.

***

I can't sleep. I am so excited I could burst. But how is this 'relationship' going to pan out? *Can we really be boyfriend and girlfriend when he's my boss and we work in the same office? Well, he's got his own office, but overall office.*

Oh I want to kiss him again. Tomorrow. Oh it seems so long away, but just tonight and one day at work and I'll be able to... Ooh...

I wake up with the alarm and realise, thankfully, that I must have drifted off whilst imagining kissing Thomas. That's the last thing I can remember thinking anyway.

***

Malcolm had a shocking night in the hostel. Although there was a policy of no noise after midnight, a few guys had decided not to adhere to it, and there had not been any staff around to sort it out. Malcolm had wanted to get up to see if he could find someone, but didn't want to be a snitch. *These guys need the shelter and who am I to tell tales on them and maybe stop them from staying here again?* He'd thought. He'd decided, *it's not the done thing*, so he'd suffered in silence. It wasn't all banter; there were groans, moans and vocalised nightmares too. He began to think that he had more peace outside on the streets, but stopped himself and remembered to be grateful for the bed and the warmth. Anyway, it wasn't quiet outside – never – it was just a noise that he'd begun to get used to. He hadn't thought about this before, and found it a little profound that this was actually the case – he was getting used to it all!

The alarm rang, which meant it was time to get up and head straight to the communal hall for breakfast. Robbie had jumped out of his bed immediately.

"Wow, you're keen!" Malcolm groaned.

"No, I'm not keen, I've hardly slept and was going stir crazy keeping quiet and still"

"Oh, you as well; I was the same"

"Hah, it's often like that in here, but at least it's warm. Let's go" Robbie said jumping up and down.

Not long after, leaving the hostel, Malcolm decided he was going to tell Robbie the truth – today…

***

Andy arrived home after his night shift, flung his keys on the kitchen table and made a cup of tea. It hadn't been a good night; one sexual attack on a young girl, a mugging and a non-fatal stabbing. How can people be so fucking bad? He didn't need to keep asking himself this question, and he wasn't looking for an answer, it was just that his empathy for victims was so high and his anger at the perpetrators' heinous crimes was almost violent. He slammed his hand down on the pine table. His tea shook and some spilled out of the mug onto the table top. He watched it trickle along the wood's natural groove.

"Hey darling, everything OK?"

He looked up, abruptly, to see his wife in the doorway, her blonde mid length hair ruffled, and her eyes narrow from sleep.

"No, it's not!" he snapped.

Jen turned on her heels and walked back upstairs slowly, choosing not to have a row right now. She knew when one was brewing in her husband so it was best to let him get on with it.

He'd never hit her, nothing like that; he was just prone to getting angry at the world.

***

Later that afternoon, after much procrastination, Malcolm broached the subject.

"Robbie?" he began.

"Yes mate? What is it?" Robbie saw that Malcolm was looking pale all of a sudden. "Are you alright?"

"Um, yes, I'm OK. I just er, I just, well, let's see, I don't know why I am stuck for words when I am a writer…"

"A writer? Oh is that what you used to be then?"

"Um, no, not exactly. It's what I AM" Malcolm studied Robbie's face, looking for his reaction. "Now" he finished.

"Now? But you can't be now, you're here with me, homeless and deranged" he laughed.

"No Robbie, that's what I've had you believe. You see, I'm writing a novel, it's my tenth novel in fact. And I wanted to show what it was like living on the streets of London in 2014. A bit like George

Orwell's 'Down and out in Paris and London' but a modern version."

Robbie's face didn't move. His mouth was slightly open, his eyes wide and he looked serious.

"Do you know the book?" Malcolm asked.

"Yes. I do. I've read it… quite a while ago now"

"Well, that's what I'm doing, and all this, this is research. I was going to tell you earlier, but then I would be getting a false you, a false sense of what life is like on these streets"

Robbie didn't seem to like this news, his eyes narrowing "So it was all bullshit? Total bullshit? So I've been helping you to write your next book? You didn't really want to be friends, you just wanted something to write about? Is that it?"

"Well, erm, not exactly, but kind of. I mean, I like you and I do feel that we've become good friends."

"Friends don't lie" Robbie interrupted.

"I know, but can't you understand what I'm…"

"Oh so, I expect you'll tell me you live in a mansion next, with a beautiful wife and 2.4 children?"

"Oh no, nothing like that Robbie. I live in a two bed semi, in a normal suburban street, I am divorced and have no children, sadly. I made that bit up too."

Robbie's face softened a little. "Oh right. So don't you make a lot of money writing then?"

"I make enough. If you mean 'why do I live in a two bed semi', it's because I choose to spend my money on other things. I'll tell you about that later"

"No, I don't think so. I think you'd better tell me now" Robbie insisted.

"OK, well, I give much of my money to charities; particularly homeless charities. That's all"

"That's all?" Robbie said in disbelief, his voice getting louder. "That's all? Oh my… oh my, oh my, oh my" Robbie shook his head slowly, trying to get to grips with what he was being told.

"I've got a spare bedroom. Would you like to come and stay with me?"

***

I positively bounce into work today. Thomas, I've decided, is not only a hunk (in my eyes) and a great lover, and a good laugh, and a gentleman, but he's also like a human form of anti-depressant. I am sure many men and women are, and Thomas just happens to be mine, but all the same, it's true. I *feel* more alive and like I have something really good going on now. I know I mustn't rely on Thomas as being my 'pick me up' as it could all go horribly wrong like it did with Dave, but I cannot help giving in to the excitement of it all and the glow that is washing over me.

Dave, mmm, now he kind of gave me that glow, but not as bright as this one, and besides, when I found out he was shagging my friend, Lisa, I not only lost the glow, but the boyfriend and friend too. In some ways I wish I'd never found out, then it wouldn't have hurt, then I wouldn't have told Lisa where to shove her *sorry*.

"Cup of tea?"

"Ooh" I'm shaken out of my daydream or rather day nightmare "Oh Janice, yes please" I smile.

Janice turns on her heels with an "Okey dokey" and heads off to the office kitchenette.

After a few seconds, I follow her.

"Oh hi, look cakes" she states pointing at several bakery boxes on the worktop "Its Robert's birthday today, so he brought in these cream donuts – are you gonna have one?"

"mmm, yes I think I will"

"Ooh being naughty today are we?" she questions, not really as a question though.

"Yes I am, and…" I tail off.

"And… what?" she asks, her eyes widening as she steps in to hear all my gossip. But it's no good, I've decided not to say anything now. I don't know what I was thinking in the first place.

"Oh nothing, let's go eat these cakes eh, bring the tea love"

"Hey you, *nothing*? Come on tell! Is it about you or someone else?"

"It's not about anyone, let's go"

"Oh that's not fair" she moans trailing behind me with two mugs of hot tea "You shouldn't start something you're not going to finish. Now I'll have to make something up"

"Now that's a good idea. It would be more interesting that way" I laugh, turning to wink at her.

We sit down, the phone rings and work starts; another busy day in the world of insurance.

I drank my tea, but I've only managed two mouthfuls of cake within the last two hours, so I've binned it, a little frustrated. That was, until I checked my emails and found one from Thomas, from an hour and five minutes ago! I've been so busy, Mr *'anti-depressant'* had actually slipped my mind. I think I'll call him AD for short. Well, in my mind, not to his face as he'll then ask me what it means and I'm so not going there.

Anyway, the email just says *Good morning, I need you to do a little filing in my office, in say, half an hour?* Oh shit, that was over half hour ago. I glance over to his office. His door is shut. I think I'd better reply; and quickly. *Good morning Mr Banks I am so sorry I got caught up with other work and didn't see your email, am I too late?* I send it. Then I check to make sure it's in my sent box, which it is, and I wait. It's only one minute, but seems like fifteen, and he's replied! *No Miss Taylor now is also fine – I just need you for half hour say, OK?* I don't hesitate and don't bother to reply, I just get up, tell Janice that I have some files to go through with the *boss* which I punctuate with my index and middle fingers, in the inverted commas mode whilst scrunching my face up as if I don't want to go and help him.

Janice buys it and says "Good luck, have fun ha ha" sarcastically.

She doesn't *know* Thomas. I hadn't before our soiree, and the general consensus in the office, which I was also party to, was that he was boring and unapproachable. Well, I now know that to be untrue, but I won't say a thing, as this way, no-one will think anything of it. I'll just play along…

…Until I enter his office and see his bright blue eyes light up, igniting what seems like a steam train in my heart. Phew! No, not a steam train, a blooming rocket!

"Ah, Miss Taylor, do take a seat" he says gesturing towards the chair opposite his at his desk.

"Ooh very formal" I grin.

"Well, we have to keep up face, Miss Taylor, my office is surrounded by windows and if I pulled all the blinds down it might raise a question or two don't you think?" he winks.

"Ooh yes Mr Banks and we don't want that!" I laugh, then add "No, seriously, it's definitely how things should be kept… at least here… at work"

He nodds. "So, I have some filing for you"

I hadn't realised he was serious about the filing and I am actually feeling a little annoyed that he really does want me to do some. I mean, I've done a lot of filing in my life, but those days are gone, and I am so much more than a filing clerk!

I must have my annoyance written all over my face, which is typical of me, being a *heart on my sleeve* girl, because he has frozen, and is now apologising that it's filing, but that he just had to see me, and it was the only way.

My face softens, as I like this idea, and I tell him that it's fine, and well worth it.

As I go through files and folders, getting them in order to add to the cabinets, he asks me about my day yesterday, probes some more into what I like doing in my spare time, and asks me my favourite foods. He seems so interested and actually listens, so it seems! I ask similar things, my priority being whether he likes football, as I cannot stand it. He doesn't. Yay!

As this conversation goes on, we busy ourselves with other things, so as to fool any potential audience outside. Crumbs, it's like we're having some sordid affair or something, behind our spouses backs, but it's not, we just like each other and want to share our bodies too, hopefully for a long time to come.

I'm actually sad when all the files are where they need to be. I wish I could have slowed down, but it's not in my nature; I tend to get on with a job, full on, until it's done.

"Is there anything else you'd like me to do?"

"Well of course, but not here" he jokes, raising his eyebrow at me with a grin.

Now that was a bit corny, but hey, I'll let him off this time.

"No seriously" he continues "that's it. I kind of had to make that job up as it was"

"What? So the files didn't even need filing?"

"Well, they were already filed, until I got my hands on them this morning…"

"Bloody cheek!" I say, just a little too harshly.

"Well, it got you in here, didn't it?" he looks like a lost puppy now.

I soften, quickly. "Yes. I was just joking – it was a great idea! Well, until tonight then; if you're still on for tonight?"

"Oh yes" he's smiling again now, thank goodness. "Eight o'clock, I'll come and pick you up, OK?"

"Yes, that's perfect! Until then…"

I turn and leave, returning to my desk with a big yawn and a humdrum style "Right, back to something much more interesting" to Janice.

She glances up and tells me it's my turn to make tea. Ha! Well lucky I'm in a good mood…

***

"I don't believe you!" Robbie finally shouted.

A few passers' by glanced their way but carried on walking.

"Shh" Malcolm snorted. "Look, I'm sorry. I'm sorry I lied to you. Well, I didn't lie really, I just bent the truth a little, but only so that I could get to know all about guys like you living on the streets, you know, why, how and so forth"

"Guys?" Robbie's eyes narrowed.

"Yes guys. You are not the first person I have kind of befriended on the streets of London, but you are the first I have asked to stay at my house" Malcolm offered tilting his head to the left, scrunching up his lips.

Robbie stared at him for a few seconds. He felt annoyed, yet inquisitive, and a tiny bit hopeful.

"OK then" he started "where do you live?"

"In Kingston upon Thames"

"Who do you live with?"

"I live alone"

"And why do you want to help the homeless?" Robbie couldn't help the sarcasm in his voice, but he didn't know whether to believe Malcolm or not at this point.

"Because…" Malcolm paused, as if he had a lump in his throat suddenly. He cleared his throat. "Because, I felt that it was the right thing for me to do when my wife left me" he finished quickly and sniffed.

Robbie continued to stare at him and finally said "OK, let's go and see this house of yours" He still didn't believe him fully, but there was something about Malcolm and the look in his eyes right now that told him he was probably telling the truth.

They took the train to Clapham Junction, another train to Kingston and then a fifteen minute walk to Malcolm's house, not saying much to each other during the whole hour. Malcolm paid the fares. A few people glanced twice at them on the journey, but there were no stares and no abuse. Only when Malcolm took a key from his front upper pocket, placed it in the keyhole, and opened the door to a semi-detached house, did Robbie believe that he might just be telling the truth. He also thought that Malcolm might be up to something else, but this thought was soon dissipated when Malcolm beckoned him into the kitchen, took out two mugs from an upper cupboard, filled the kettle with water, plugged it in and set it to boil. It was all too familiar to be a hoax.

"So there's not going to be a "You've been hoaxed' or something with film camera's then?" Robbie laughed.

"Ha! No, sorry, it's just me and my home mate"

"Oh good, I didn't really feel dressed for the occasion anyway"

Malcolm lent over to Robbie and patted him heartily on his back "Welcome to my abode" he announced "Do you take sugar in your tea?"

***

Seven o'clock and he'll be at mine in an hour! Shit! Blooming delays, I'm getting sick of them! So, let's think, according to the board, I should be at the station at 7.30, so home by 7.45; shit, just fifteen minutes to get ready! No! Perhaps I should put him back a little. Is there time? Best find out.

I text him Hi Thomas! I'm not home yet! A delay on the train! If you haven't left yet, can you come half hour later? X

Oh blow, why didn't I just phone him? Everything is blooming texts these days; I cannot believe I am now a part of all that!

Bing!

Oh blow, what's he got to say?

Hi Sophie, no worries at all, I hope you are OK, trains eh! I will pick you up at 8.30. Any probs, just let me know x

Oh good – I knew he was a gentleman!

***

I feel a bit flustered now but still excited. I was hoping to have a long hot bath, a face pack and general pampering before my 'date' but there was no time. I had a quick shower instead, threw my clothes on, and put most of my efforts into my hair and a little make up. After all, at dinner, it will be mostly my face he'll be looking at. Or at least I hope he'll be looking at me. As long as he's not one of those men who have wandering eyes…

I look in the mirror, carefully applying my mascara, head tilted back, looking down into the mirror, brushing black liquid through my eyelashes, and I realise I am talking to myself. I am chatting, in fact, like I have a friend there, but I am alone.

I stop for a moment and remind myself out loud "They say that people who talk to themselves are a bit mad" but I scrunch my face up and tell myself "Well, I think we're all a bit mad anyway, so who cares?" I shrug my shoulders and continue with my make-up applications.

Bruno comes to sit with me, purring, so I spend a couple of minutes stroking him. He's my best friend and I tell him so every day.

The door bells rings and I nearly jump out of my seat. "Oh my gosh, it's him!"

"Coming!" I shout, although he won't be able to hear me anyway. I look at my clock – crumbs he's bang on time. Well, reliability is a good thing.

His beaming face is a picture as I open the door, and I feel a flutter in my tummy as he bends in to kiss me on the lips. Mmm, those soft, full lips! I invite him in and he says that he will turn his motor off in that case, and bounces off down the path, his pert little bottom wiggling slightly as he went. I couldn't help but notice.

"Oh don't worry" I call after him "I'm ready, I'll come now" I grab my keys from the hall table and run out of the house.

***

"Ooh it's a lovely restaurant; Thai food is one of my favourites" I tell him as we are seated.

"Great, I was hoping you would like it as it was a bit of a risk" he smiles "So, tonight we can get to know each other better – I have lots of questions"

I realise I am most likely blushing as I giggle, thinking of how well we already know each other's bodies whilst knowing very little about each other's lives or personalities.

"Well" I say finally "Be my guest. I hope to learn all about you too!"

We order wine and water, and he makes a start with his questions straight away "So, where were you born?"

***

A few miles away, Malcolm and Robbie were having tea and beans on toast. Malcolm didn't have much food in, given the circumstances, so suggested they could go shopping a bit later on, after a shower and a change of clothes. Robbie washed first, luxuriating in the warm stream of the power shower, soaking up the sweet smells of the shower gel and shampoo as he lathered his hair and body, and rinsed it all off. As he looked down, the water was brownish which made him feel sad and he began to sob about the state he'd gotten himself into on the streets, the kindness shown by Malcolm and this unbelievable situation of now being at Malcolm's house where he has been offered a bed and food. It seemed so surreal he actually pinched himself and was glad to acknowledge that it did hurt.

He lathered up again and rinsed until the water was clear, then stepped out and wrapped himself in the cream fluffy towel that Malcolm had laid out for him. Rubbing his hair with a hand towel, he walked over to the bathroom cabinet mirror and studied his face. He would have to do something about that beard, but he was looking refreshed, albeit the bags under his eyes were dark and his skin quite rough. He pulled on the pants and clothes that Malcolm had laid out for him, and wandered downstairs, waiting for a reaction from his new friend and well, he guessed, landlord.

"Oh mate, you scrubbed up well! Feeling better after that?"

"Oh yes, thank you, it was a beautiful shower"

"Good. Right, I'd better get sorted as well and then we can go out. Help yourself to tea or whatever you can find in the cupboards and the remote controls to the TV are on the arm of the sofa, if you fancy a bit of TV. There's probably a lot more channels since you last used a TV, due to *freeview*, but I will give you the low down on all that later. See you in a bit then"

"OK, will do"

Robbie went straight into the lounge and slumped down on the sofa. It was even more comfortable than it looked, all soft and... Robbie went straight to sleep as soon as his head sank into a cushion.

"Wakey wakey, mate" Malcolm was saying gently, whilst shaking Robbie lightly.

"Eh, ooh, oh" Robbie was a bit stunned, but woke quickly. "Oh wow" he continued "I was just dreaming that this was all a dream!"

Malcolm laughed "Ah, no, it's not a dream, it's all really happening"

And within five minutes, they were off to the supermarket armed with a shopping list Malcolm had compiled. He'd written it whilst letting Robbie have a few more minutes asleep after he'd found him crashed out on the sofa. He didn't really want to wake him up but thought it would be best to get him straight into his new life, so that he felt at home.

All the fruit was laid out neatly in the supermarket and looked so appetising, Robbie chose apples, oranges and raspberries; adding them to the trolley Malcolm was pushing round.

***

So, we are onto the dessert now, and what a wonderful evening we've had. I have learnt that Thomas has a younger brother, Jonathan, who he hasn't seen for some time and an older sister, Liz, who I'd already met at his house. He is thirty three and lives alone. He has never been married and has no children, and he loves to go out, have fun and enjoy a few holidays. And he now knows that I am twenty eight, am an only child, love my music and non-fiction books, documentaries, films and theatre. He also shares those interests, but his style of music is quite different – I am a pop girl and he's more a rock man. But, that aside, I'm sure if we went to a music festival, there would be something for both of us to enjoy. *Best not look too far ahead, Sophie!* I berated myself silently.

Thomas has had two long term relationships, apparently, but they both ran their course, and neither were wife material, so they'd agreed to go their separate ways. He doesn't see either of them now, but the splits were both amicable. He doesn't like one night stands, never has, and is definitely looking for Mrs Right. Well, that's all nice to hear, I must say, and I am glad I wasn't a one night stand!

I told him of my tumultuous relationship with Brian when I was young, and how his wayward ways, hapless motorcycle riding with me on the back, and all the parties, had once been desirable to me, but that I had grown up eventually and he never did. He also got into drugs and I had called it a day when I found out. I also told him about Dave.

I didn't go into the details about any other boyfriends, but said that I had been single for the past year, enjoyed my own company, and felt independent, but that it would be lovely to be in a loving relationship now; someone to travel with, and just hang out with; nothing too serious, but if it headed that way, I wouldn't be scared of commitment. I thought that sounded good but not too desperate, and anyway, I am *not* desperate.

We chatted about holidays, and it turns out that we were both in Egypt the same year, and have both been to Turkey and Australia. Apart from that, we have chosen differing destinations; him Italy to my Spain, Morocco to my Bulgaria, Czechoslovakia to my Holland, and Venice to my Thailand. But we've both skied, and enjoyed it, so that's a good thing. Maybe we'll go together sometime? I'd love to go again.

He's now getting dressed as I lie in bed naked watching him in the dim light of the side lamp. "How long will it take you to drive home?" I ask him.

"Oh, only around fifteen minutes at this time of night" he smiles. "I'd love to stay, but I can't, I have some stuff to pick up from home"

"You weren't very organised then!" I tease.

"Well, I couldn't be too sure that there would be an invite to stay" he smiles.

"Hee hee, OK, I'll let you off – maybe next time…"

My gosh he's so fit, I cannot believe I've been working for him for the last two years, and yet had never noticed him as anything special, but now I see him like some sort of Adonis. He seems to like me too; he kept touching my hand over the table at the restaurant, even lifted it and kissed it one time. He seems so gentle too; in personality and in the bedroom. I feel like I'm in a dream.

Fully dressed, he bends over me to kiss me goodbye, and I quickly get up, snog him deeply, put my dressing gown on and tell him I must see him out. "Not that I want you to leave, mind…"

Shutting the door behind him, I jump up and down a few times like a young child and do a silent excited scream. *Oh my, life is good!*

I received a letter in the post this morning for my mental health assessment. I guess I will still go, but I am feeling so much better now, I will have to tell them that I have improved. *Maybe the doctor is right, though, and some talking therapy will do me good.*

***

Thomas drove off with a smile on his face that stayed there for some minutes. He put on a Coldplay CD, and thought about his second date with Sophie. *Such a pretty girl, and so genuine. I think I'm falling in love already; how can that be? But she makes my heart flutter and I haven't felt like that for a long time. And she's interesting, loves to travel and go out to the theatre and all sorts. She likes to chat, but also listens and she is as close to me as I am to her. Oh and films; I can imagine us at mine, cuddled up on the sofa after I've cooked dinner, watching movies, especially on a Sunday after lunch...* Chris Martin singing 'Para-paradise' from the car speakers' jolted him from his thoughts, and he felt like it was exactly the word to describe his bedroom activities with Sophie.

"Paradise. Mmm" he said out loud. "Woohoo!"

***

It had been a few days since Andy saw Malcolm and he hoped he was OK as thoughts of him sprang to mind during his morning tea making process. *Maybe he's got a shelter*, he thought, and hoped. But, for Andy, it was business as usual, and not all about walking the streets looking out for the homeless. On the contrary, he was usually in a car, with a partner, chasing crime; rapists, murderers, robbers, drug dealers… He shuddered, just thinking about it. He'd had enough of the job, but he couldn't just leave and he knew that his dissatisfaction was partly because he was unhappy at home.

Jen said she's going to get look into getting some therapy as well. I hope she does. I cannot be to blame for everything that goes wrong and for the unhappiness of both of us. We've been on/off since I can remember, breaking up every couple of months and then carrying on, even before the girls were born or even thought about. Can we really give up on this marriage? I feel like I can now, as I think we've tried too many times, but then I'm still not sure that we have really tried; more like just carried on as we were and repeated everything all over again.

We shall see. I need to have some closure on this soon. I cannot stand it, as it is, much longer.

He felt more ready to face the day as he got in his car and drove off to work.

***

Robbie woke after ten hours sleep. He hadn't had more than four hours at a time for many years, and he could barely believe it when he stumbled downstairs and Malcolm greeted him and told him of his marathon sleep. Malcolm made him tea and said he'd waited for him to wake before having breakfast so that they could eat together. Given three options for breakfast, Robbie took about a minute to choose one; he hadn't had porridge, toast or bacon for a long time and greedily thought that he'd like all three. He opted for a toasted bacon sandwich and devoured it, washed down with hot steaming tea.

"I was thinking" Robbie said "how come your house was so warm when we got here, and you had hot water when you were presumably away for a few weeks?"

"Ah, well I left a key with a good friend of mine, Peter, as he offered to check on the place occasionally and I called him a few days before I planned to come home, so that he could turn the heating up and make sure we had hot water ready. I've been living on the streets for nearly three months, so I needed a good shower too!" he smiled.

***

Halfway through the morning at work, Liz called Thomas on his mobile. "Hi sis" he greeted her "how's it going?"

"Ah good thanks, are you OK to talk?"

"Yes, I've got a few minutes for you anyway"

"Aw, that's nice. I just had some good news I wanted to share. I've just been offered a new job, working in the Tottenham YMCA! I am so excited; I cannot wait to help the vulnerable youngsters staying there!"

"Wow, that's amazing sis, I didn't even know you were going for a new job?"

"I know, I didn't want to say in case I didn't get it; I didn't want to jinx it"

"Ah! You and your superstitions! Do you still salute a single magpie?" he laughed.

"Yes, I do actually! Although I didn't see any in Africa ha ha"

"No, I don't suppose you did! So, what is the job and when do you start?"

"Team Manager; and I start next Monday!" Liz' voice raised higher the more excited she got. "So… I wondered if you are available tonight for a celebratory drink; just the two of us?"

"Yes, of course, I have no plans so I'll come and pick you up… actually, no if we are having a drink, then I had better get a taxi and we can go from there – my treat sis, all night, no arguments, and I will be round at 8pm, OK?"

"OK, sounds lovely to me – I'll see you then! Have a lovely afternoon!"

"You too! Bye bye!"

"Byeee"

***

I've relaxed tonight, with a Chinese takeaway, *EastEnders*, a few documentaries on crime that I've recorded, a couple of glasses of red wine and some chamomile tea before bed. I am only part way through the first chapter of my new romance kindle book, but I cannot keep my eyes open any longer, so I turn my side lamp off ready to sleep.

***

In the same evening, Robbie and Malcolm chatted a little about Malcolm's book, which is apparently going to share the truth about poverty and homeless in London by telling the stories of people he met. Robbie became rather interested and offered to give Malcolm more insights and thoughts on it all in return for his kindness of having him stay with him. Malcolm was delighted and made a lasagne and salad for their dinner, which they ate whilst watching *EastEnders* and news.

Malcolm then told Robbie that he was a journalist for years, working for newspapers and then magazines, but that when he went freelance, he found it too much of a struggle, so began writing a blog about important stuff such as the homeless, poverty, abuse, and working class problems. The blog then led to the idea of writing a book, and hopefully more in the future. His previous books are all science fiction, so it's something very different; more similar to his journalism.

Robbie was a little put off when hearing of this background, but softened because he could see, and knew inside from their time together in the past, that Malcolm was genuine and was doing what he was doing, and had done what he'd done, for all the right reasons.

***

Thomas and Liz had a lovely evening with a little champagne and a Mexican meal, a whole lot of banter about her new job and, as always, a little about their brother; their brother they wish they could see.

***

Andy had been chatting to Jen who had finally agreed to go to marriage counselling. She had even found some places they could try. Andy had been left thinking that he would need to stop his group therapy in order to do the marriage counselling, but his family meant a lot more to him than himself, rightly or wrongly.

***

Oh what a night for everyone!

***

The week went on with Robbie settling in at Malcolm's home, trying to understand his kindness. Malcolm was feeling very enlightened by his new guest. Thomas and I have had two more dates and I am a very happy bunny, and Liz starts her new job this sunny Monday morning…

***

Liz' first day at work was like many others' first days – lots of introductions to people whose names she'd have forgotten by the time she was introduced to the next person if she hadn't have been taking notes, lots of cups of tea, a session on the computer to set her up with her password and show her how the system worked, and a tour of the building; fire exits, toilets etc. She would be in training for a time, because although she'd worked in this field before for the youth homeless sector, and overseeing schooling projects for needy families with children in Africa, she would be looking after quite a number of staff.

Liz travelled home exhausted but very happy. She knew she'd love the job and the people working there - she had sensed it. She'd made a few notes throughout the day and took another look at them on the train to refresh her memory. She couldn't wait to help make a positive difference in many homeless youngsters' lives in London.

***

Robbie stayed in all day with Malcolm, reading through articles Malcolm had written and had published in newspapers and magazines, and photos of Malcolm and his late mum and dad (both passed due to cancer; breast and bowel) who he'd cherished and helped to care for, in part, when they needed it. They also drank lots of cups of tea.

"One of the best Great British traditions; tea drinking!" exclaimed Malcolm carrying the fourth mug of the day into the lounge. Slumped on the huge, beige, fabric sofa they continued looking at photos, this time from the photo album on Malcolm's laptop.

"So, who is that lady?" asked Robbie with a smirk at a photo of Malcolm kissing a dark haired lady on the cheek.

"Oh, that's Melanie, my girlfriend of two years" he quickly moved onto the next photo.

"Two years? So, what happened?"

"She had an affair and me being me, out and about a lot, bumped into her, and him, having a romantic lunch, holding hands over the table in a hotel restaurant"

"Oh" Robbie finally said after a few seconds pause. He could find no other words, so instead asked Malcolm where the next photo was taken. Apparently, it was him and his mum in Hyde Park of all places!

***

Thomas and I managed to finish work a little early today, as Thomas wanted to surprise me with something. We travelled to the embankment on the tube and as we walked along the embankment in the sun, chatting and laughing, he grabbed me gently, pulled me to him, told me "I really like you – a lot!" and kissed me hard on the lips with a little groan. This turned into a snog and I felt like I was walking on air…

Right now, it's like walking on air in another way I guess. Yes, Thomas is kissing me again with those super lips of his, but it's not that; we are at the top of the London Eye, in a capsule, 135 metres above the ground. We have champagne and chocolates (*Hotel Chocolat*, my favourite!) being served by our private host, who answers any questions we have. But, we are very wrapped up in ourselves, thank you very much, and we have fun spotting as much as we can recognise from our own knowledge. The Champagne is going to my head a little, but it's all good; I feel fantastic.

I feel very lucky as I stand with Thomas, holding his hand, gazing out across London. He arranged this all for me. How romantic! No-one has ever made a gesture anything like this before. In fact, Dave taking me to the zoo as a surprise for my birthday was the most romantic, but then he did get free tickets as he won them in a competition he'd entered.

Anyway, no time to think about that, I must stay 'in the moment' and enjoy this, right here, right now, today; with Thomas. Bliss.

"Oh, I've made a reservation for dinner too; a lovely little Italian restaurant I think you'll like".

"Sounds wonderful, Thomas" I reply, and kiss him again.

***

By Wednesday, Liz was getting settled into her new job, taking in everything she could from the acting Team Manager who was training her, when an incident occurred, involving a young girl staying at the hostel and a pen knife. She'd cut herself, badly, on the wrists.

It was a reality check for Liz, but she wasn't fazed and dealt with the girl, the ambulance and then the police. And that is when she got a surprise.

"Oh my word, it's you! Andy!" she'd exclaimed as Andy walked in. She gave him a kiss, and then got on with the matter in hand, which was very serious and her priority of course.

Once everything had been reported, and before Liz could think about visiting the girl in hospital, Andy asked after her brother.

"Oh he's as adorable as ever. And he has a new girlfriend! I am so pleased for him!"

"Good stuff. Well, how about we meet up for a drink sometime, or even a meal, and ask Thomas along?"

"Yes, that would be great. I'll call him later"

They exchanged mobile phone numbers and Liz said she'd call him the next day, after chatting to Thomas.

"Friday might be good" said Andy "If you're free?"

"Well, I am actually, so hopefully Thomas will be too. I must go now, I'll call you tomorrow" she'd said, walking away hurriedly.

"Great! Bye. And I hope the girl is all good"

***

Incident dealt with, the girl was thankfully stable, had received a few stitches, and was regretting her impulsive actions, promising she'd never do it again. She also agreed to take part properly in her counselling sessions from then on.

Liz left the hospital and phoned Thomas.

"Thomas, you're not going to believe who I bumped into today!"

"OK, who?"

"Andy. Andy Dulamain"

"Andy? Wow, I haven't seen him in years! Is he OK?"

"Yes, I think so. And he's a policeman with the Met, how about that?"

"Mmm, well I expect that job suits him; he has a kind heart but believes in law and order"

"Indeed. I kept picturing us as kids, all hanging out after school. He was both of our best friends wasn't he; a great trio we made"

"Ah yes, and so long ago it seems now"

"Yes! It was, and the time goes so quickly…"

"So, did you get his number?"

"Oh yes, and he has mine. He wondered, actually, if we'd like to go for dinner with him on Friday – can you come?"

"Um, let's think… No, no I can't, I've made arrangements with Sophie; I wouldn't want to let her down"

"No, of course not. Well, how about you bring her along? Do you think she'd be OK with that?"

"Yes. Yes I think she will be fine with it; she's a very lovely girl"

"Great! Well, I shall hang up now, dear brother, and phone him to confirm. I'll let you know what time and where OK?"

"Yep, that's fine. Speak to you later sis"

"Will do"

She quickly called Andy's number. He answered on the second ring. "Hello, Andy speaking" he said in a low, manly voice.

"Hi Andy, its Liz"

"Hey, hi Liz!"

"You mentioned dinner on Friday, so I just spoke to Thomas and he can come. He will bring his new girlfriend with him, as he'd already made arrangements to see her on Friday, so there will be four of us. She's a sweet girl; you'll like her"

"Good stuff. So, how about I meet you all at 8pm in the Mango Tree – it's a Thai restaurant on Grosvenor Place, do you know it?"

"Mmm, Thai, I haven't had Thai for a long time! I have been there once, yes; it's a great restaurant"

"Well that's a done deal then. 8pm Friday"

"Yes, and I look forward to it very much. See you then and we can catch up properly"

"See you then, Liz, have a nice evening"

***

Friday came round quickly for everyone.

***

I have been very much looking forward to going out tonight, as I'm going out for dinner with Thomas, his sister and an old friend of theirs. I really want to get to know Liz and am so pleased to have been made a part of Thomas' life so quickly. Other boyfriends have been very withholding when it came to making me a part of their friends or families, so I am falling in love with Thomas very quickly!

We are in a cab, holding hands and Thomas is telling me a little about his old friend, Andy, who he and his sister have known since school. He has two small children now, who Thomas has not met yet, but they had such fun when they were young, enjoying the cinema, walks, games and lots of banter between them. Thomas looks down at his hands, so I ask him if he's OK and he says he is, but there's a tinge of sadness there, I feel sure. Men often don't want to speak about their feelings as much as many women do, so I leave it at that, and change the subject, saying that I am sure we'll have a lovely evening and wonder what we might eat tonight.

"Well it's Thai food, so I'm sure it'll be good" Thomas confirms.

"Yum!"

As we reach the restaurant, stopping right outside, Thomas pays the taxi driver, gives him a tip and we say thanks as we shut the door. Thomas opens the restaurant door for me. *He's such a gentleman* I gush to myself.

We are greeted at the reception by two pretty Thai ladies, dressed in traditional Thai costume, Thomas tells her his name and she ushers us to follow her to our table, and as we near it, I see Liz sitting chatting to a bald headed man of about forty two, who is smiling and engrossed in their conversation.

"Hey, good evening guys!" greets Thomas, and Liz and the man look up, stop their chat and say their hearty hellos to us. I am introduced to Andy, who stands to kiss me on both cheeks, and he and Thomas share a hug and a pat on the back which lasts a few seconds. They look very happy to see each other.

Greetings all done, we sit down at the round table. I'm between Thomas and Andy, and opposite Liz. She's a very pretty girl with long tousled blonde highlighted hair; very slim and beautifully dressed in a figure hugging black number with stylish silver jewellery.

We are given menus and order our drinks. Liz and Andy already have a drink each, but we decide to share a bottle of white wine together to be getting on with and some sparkling water.

"So, what have you been up to?" starts Andy, but I have to excuse myself to use the ladies room, and walk off to find them.

As I do, I see Malcolm, or someone who looks remarkably like Malcolm at a table on the way to the ladies. *No, it can't be him* I tell myself *Malcolm is on the streets out there somewhere* but as I reach his table, there is no mistaking his face. I blink but he's still there. He's with another man, and they are eating already. I choose to go to the toilet, and try to work out how this can be; how he can be dining in here when I've seen him on the streets being moved on by the police.

As I pass their table again I decide not to say anything to him, as I cannot even think of what I would say *Oh hello, didn't I see you on the streets a couple of weeks ago being moved on by the police?* No, I don't think so. So I sit back down with my little group and join in with the conversation which has now turned to Andy's job – as a policeman.

But I cannot stop thinking about Malcolm and I tell Andy about the man called Malcolm who I saw on the streets who is now in here. He says he has no idea how that could be, that he also knows of someone on the streets called Malcolm, and that maybe it is just someone who looks remarkably like him. I agree that this is the most plausible answer, and try to forget about it. We order our food, which I am very excited about as Thai food reminds me of some wonderful experiences in Thailand. Food and memories; they just go together.

A short while later, Andy goes to the toilet He seems to have been gone quite a while when I look round after him, and I notice he is over chatting to Malcolm and the man Malcolm is with. Gosh, I hope everything is OK. Andy can't move him on from a restaurant can he? I mean he is dressed well now; not like he was when I last saw him.

But, before I can open my mouth to say anything to Thomas, I see that Andy is walking back to our table. As he reaches us, he looks a little shaken and pale.

"Thomas, Liz, there's something I need to tell you" he starts.

"Oh my, Andy, is everything OK?" Thomas butts in.

"Um, yes, yes I'm OK. You were right Sophie, it is Malcolm from the streets" he tells me.

Then he sits down, reaches over to take Liz and Thomas' hands and continues "It's your brother, Robbie; he's just over there with a man called Malcolm, and he wants to say hello."

THE END

"Relationships are like flowers – they bloom, then the petals fall off, one by one, and we need to make new buds grow into new flowers."

***

About the Author

Well, instead of telling you all about me here, you can find all about me and my latest news through my blog/website or various social networks:

Blog/website:

http://www.amandagreenauthor.co.uk

Facebook:

https://www.facebook.com/AmandaGreenAuthor

Twitter: https://twitter.com/AmandaGreenUK

Goodreads:

https://www.goodreads.com/AmandaGreenAuthorUK

I am also on LinkedIn, AuthorsDB and many other sites.

Other books by Amanda Green

Memoirs

'My Alien Self: My Journey Back to Me'

(Memoirs of Amanda Green) available as

paperback and kindle ebook

And

'39' (Memoirs of Amanda Green)

Short story books

'What I Know and two more short stories'

(Amanda Green's Short Stories)

And

'The Woman Who Lives Next Door – A Short Story (Amanda Green's Short Stories)

Novelette

'Living The Dream – A Novelette (An Amanda Green Novelette)

Made in the USA
Charleston, SC
21 March 2016